GW00371036

The Way People Are

A NEW WINDMILL BOOK OF VIEWPOINTS ON SOCIETY

Edited by John O'Connor

Heinemann
New Windmills

Heinemann Educational Publishers
Halley Court, Jordan Hill, Oxford OX2 8EJ
A division of Reed Educational and Professional Publishing Ltd

OXFORD MELBOURNE AUCKLAND
JOHANNESBURG BLANTYRE GABORONE
IBADAN PORTSMOUTH (NH) USA CHICAGO

04 03
10 9 8 7 6 5 4 3 2

ISBN 0435 12531 1

Atlantic Syndication for *The Mother Tongue*, published by William Morrow, 1990; *Notes
from A Big Country* (Doubleday, 1998); *The Lost Continent,* published in *Night and Day
Magazine*. BBC Education for *The Routes of English* by Simon Elmes, published by BBC
Education, 2000; reproduced by permission of the publisher. A.M. Heath for 'The
Sporting Spirit' and 'A Sniper In The Trenches' from The *Collected Journals, Essays and
Letters of George Orwell Volumes 1-4* © George Orwell, 1945; reproduced by permission
of A.M. Heath & Co Ltd on behalf of Bill Hamilton as the Literary Executor of the Estate
of the late Sonia Brownwell Orwell and Martin Secker & Warburg Ltd. David Higham
Associates for *My Sister and Myself: The Diaries of J.R. Ackerley* by Francis King;
published by Hutchinson, 1982. The *Independent* for 'Snakes and Nutters' by Adrian
Turpin, published in the *Independent on Sunday* 9/7/00; reproduced by permission of
the *Independent*. Lawrence & Wishart for *Unemployed Struggles* by Wal Hannington,
© Lawrence & Wishart, London 1997 (first published 1936). Macmillan Publishers for
Quest For The Lost World by Brian Blessed (Boxtree, 1999) and *On Top Of The World* by
Rebecca Stephens (Macmillan, 1994); reproduced by permission of the publisher.
Penguin Books Ltd for *I Dreamed of Africa* by Kuki Gallman, © Kuki Gallman 1991,
published by Viking, 1991. Robson Books for *Cockney Rabbit* by Ray Puxley, published by
Robson Books, 1992; reproduced by permission of the publisher. Nina Slingsby Smith for
Memoirs of a Gentleman's Gentleman, published by Jonathan Cape, 1984; reproduced
by permission of the author.

Illustrations by Jackie Hill at 320 Design: 'Death of an Elephant' – Alan Baker; 'Spoken
Misprints' and 'Mississipi' – Martin Chatterton; 'Rabbitting' – Hashim Akib; 'Snakes and
Nutters' – Chloe March; 'Factory Child' – Kim Harley

Photos: John Peel – Camera Press; Ronnie Barker – BBC Photograph Library; still from
Blackadder Goes Forth – BBC Photograph Library; skydivers – Camera Press; Mount
Everest – Corbis; Emmeline Pankhurst – Corbis ; National Unemployed Workers'
Movement's March – Hulton Getty; Martin Luther King – Hulton Getty; George Orwell –
Corbis ; Bill Bryson – Camera Press/Trevor Leighton

Cover design by PCP Design Consultancy
Cover photograph by Rex Features
Typeset by Tek-Art, Croydon, Surrey
Printed and bound in the United Kingdom by Clays Ltd, St Ives PLC

Contents

Introduction for students

The extracts in this book all come under the heading of non-fiction. This means that, unlike novels and short stories, which are made-up fiction, these are true accounts from real people. When Kuki Gallman writes about witnessing the shooting of a majestic elephant, for example, she is describing a real-life experience; and the crash-landing in the South American forest related by film actor Brian Blessed really did happen.

Of course, not all of the extracts are about life-and-death dramas. You can read some of the embarrassing slip-ups uttered by sports commentators; enjoy Bill Bryson's complaints about barbers; or share the exhilaration of a free-fall jump.

The activities at the end of each section are to help you understand the extracts a little better and find new ways of looking at them. By the end you should have your own opinions about the many different kinds of writing which explore 'the way people are'.

John O'Connor

Introduction for teachers

The revised National Curriculum for English includes the requirement for students to engage with a range of 'non-fiction and non-literary texts'. The National Curriculum divides this category into four areas, one of which is personal record and viewpoints on society. *The Way People Are* has been designed to meet the needs of this requirement.

The extracts included in this collection have been carefully selected to interest and motivate Key Stage 3 students. The anthology is in two parts. In the first part the extracts have been arranged according to theme. Students can therefore compare the experiences of writers who have grown up in different cultures, for example, or explore several varying perspectives on the English language. The second part offers a selection of extracts from two observers of people and their behaviour. The two writers, George Orwell and Bill Bryson, are equally perceptive but totally different in outlook.

Following each section is a wide range of activities. These are tailored to explore each extract in line with the demands of the proposed Framework for Teaching English at Key Stage 3. There are also activities that allow for comparative work across the selection of extracts within a section.

Care has been taken to build in differentiation within each section. This is provided through the subject matter (from sports commentators' slip-ups to an eyewitness report of the 1932 Hunger March); the varying difficulty of language (from popular websites to nineteenth-century prose); and in the activities themselves.

I hope you will find that *The Way People Are* is a valuable resource in helping to meet the non-fiction requirements for all your Key Stage 3 students.

John O'Connor

People and places

The places that people inhabit have a powerful influence on them, helping to make them what they are. Someone who has grown up in the highlands of Scotland has a very different view of the world from that of a Londoner, or a person brought up in the streets of Belfast. And all of those will be different again from the viewpoint of the aboriginal Australian or Ghanaian villager. The extracts in this section all show how people's lives are shaped by the places in which they live.

Death of an elephant
Kuki Gallman

Kuki Gallman was born in Italy, but as a child always dreamed of going to Africa. When she was twenty-five she went to Kenya with her friend, Paolo, in an attempt to recover from a serious road accident. In this extract she describes an incident from a safari that they went on together. Paolo wanted to hunt and kill one of the huge elephants, a 'hundred-pounder'. Despite Kuki's arguments that this was pointless and cruel, the safari went on, and after a few days Paolo had the opportunity to fulfil his ambition.

One afternoon, finally, unexpectedly, we came across three elephants feeding up-wind. One was a large male with thick if not too long tusks, the largest sighted so far; the others, his two younger **askaris**.

The hunter nodded to Paolo. Paolo looked at Colin in offer, but he shook his head: the bull was obviously not a hundred-pounder . . . perhaps a seventy, eighty?

I think Paolo was growing tired of what must have seemed even to him a pointless search. He could see I was not happy. Perhaps I should not have joined the party in the first place, but I wanted to be with Paolo, and, of course, I was curious about any adventure which promised to be out of the ordinary.

Paolo looked briefly at me: I shook my head vigorously. We both turned to the elephant, no more than fifty metres away, who, **intermittently** flapping his ears, ignored us and kept quietly feeding from the nearby bushes.

Now and again he shook his large grey head. Then he turned towards us, undisturbed and unseeing, aware of our presence but, not being able to smell us, unbothered by it. I saw Paolo's jaw harden in determination, and my heart skipped a beat. On soft quick feet he approached the elephant, and I could only follow him closely out into the open, looking up at the grey powerful mass and feeling **vulnerable**. Paolo put the gun to his shoulders and aimed.

The elephant looked at him with alert ears. I protected my own ears with my hands: I knew the shattering blast of the .458.

The air exploded, dazzling the flies and lizards, and the old bull lifted his head backwards abruptly, tusks pointed to the sky, without a sound.

For a few instants there was just this stillness. Then he collapsed, a majestic tree stricken by lightning.

---

askaris: 'soldier' elephants
intermittently: now and then
vulnerable: able to be hurt

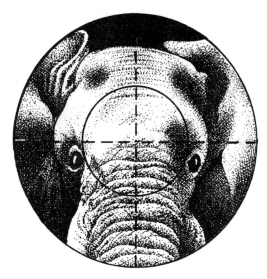

Nobody breathed: my heart beat wildly. Everything was suspended, as in a soundless slow-motion film. His companions, stunned and **uncomprehending**, searched the air for explanation with extended trunks, trumpeted furiously, opened their ears wide in a mock charge, then unexpectedly turned away **in unison** and disappeared, crashing through the bush.

Paolo started running towards the elephant for the *coup de grâce*, with me at his heels. When we reached him, we could see that a round dark hole had sprouted, like a small evil flower, in the middle of his forehead.

It had been an accurate brain shot: but the elephant is the largest animal to tread the earth. His big brain takes some time to die. I could see one of his eyes, so close that I could easily have touched it, brown-yellow, large and transparent, fringed with straight, dusty, very long

---

uncomprehending: not understanding

in unison: together

coup de grâce: the final 'mercy blow', to end the animal's suffering

eyelashes. The pupil was black and mobile. He was looking at me. I looked into that eye, and as in a mirror, I saw a smaller image of myself reflected, straight, in khaki shorts. I felt even smaller, realizing with shame and shock that I was the last thing he saw. It seemed to me there was an expression of hurt surprise in his dying yellow eye, and with all my heart, I tried to communicate to him my sorrow and my **solidarity**, and to ask his forgiveness.

A large white tear swelled up from the lower lid and rolled down his cheek, leaving a dark wet trail. The lid fluttered gently. He was dead.

I swung around to face Paolo, my own eyes full of tears, a knot of rage and shame blocking my throat. 'What right . . .' He was watching me.

The hunter came up and patted his back as was the custom. 'Well done. A clean brain shot. Congratulations.' Paolo kept watching me. As so often happened with us, that special link was established, and the rest of the world had **receded**, as if only he and I were left in it. And the elephant.

My eyes were glaring. Suddenly, his became sad and weary. He shook his head as if to cancel the scene of which we were part. 'No more,' he said, 'No more, I promise. This is my last elephant.' It was also his first.

Luka was sharpening his knife. The car was miles away and together we went to fetch it. When we came back, we found that the two younger askaris had returned and in blind fury had destroyed bushes and small trees around their friend, and covered his body gently with green branches.

I spoke no more that day. Paolo was strangely quiet. In the dark of the night, just before sleep, I remembered that an elephant had killed his brother.

---

solidarity: friendship; being on someone's side
receded: moved into the distance

My Place
Sally Morgan

Daisy Corunna was an aboriginal Australian who was born in the 1890s. As a child she lived as a servant on a white Australian's homestead, Corunna Downs Station, from which she took her surname. Here she describes some incidents from her childhood.

When I got older, my jobs on Corunna changed. They started me working at the main house, sweeping the **verandahs**, emptying the toilets, scrubbing the tables and pots and pans and the floor. In those days, you scrubbed everything. In the mornings, I had to clean the **hurricane lamps**, then help in the kitchen.

There were always poisonous snakes hiding in the dark corners of the kitchen. You couldn't see them, but you could hear them. Ssss, ssss, ssss, they went. Just like that. We cornered them and killed them with sticks. There were a lot of snakes on Corunna.

Once I was working up the main house, I wasn't allowed down in the camp. If I had've known that, I'd have stayed where I was. I couldn't sleep with my mother now and I wasn't allowed to play with all my old friends.

That was the worst thing about working at the main house, not seeing my mother every day. I knew she missed me. She would walk up from the camp and call, 'Daisy, Daisy', just like that. I couldn't talk to her, I had too much work to do. It was hard for me, then. I had to sneak away just to see my own family and friends. They were camp natives, I was a house native.

---

verandahs: covered terraces along the sides of a house
hurricane lamps: lamps designed to stand up to high winds

Now, I had to sleep on the **homestead** verandah. Some nights, it was real cold, one blanket was too thin. On nights like that, the natives used to bring wool from the shearing shed and lay that beneath them.

I didn't mind sleeping on the verandah in summer because I slept near the old cooler. It was as big as a fireplace, they kept butter and milk in it. I'd wait till everyone was asleep, then I'd sneak into the cooler and pinch some butter. I loved it, but I was never allowed to have any.

Seems like I was always getting into trouble over food. I'm like a lamb that's never been fed. I 'member once, Nell asked me to take an apple pie to the house further out on the station. Nell's real name is Eleanor, but everyone called her Nell. Anyway, I kept walkin' and walkin' and smellin' that pie. Ooh, it smelled good. I couldn't stand it any longer, I hid in a gully and dug out a bit of pie with my fingers. It was beautiful. I squashed the pie together and tried to make out like it was all there. Hmmmnnn, that was good **tucker**, I said to myself as I walked on.

When I gave the pie to Mrs Stone, I had to give her a note that Nell had sent as well. If I had have known what was in that note, I'd have thrown it away. It said, if any part of this pie is missing, send the note back and I will punish her.

Mrs Stone looked at the note, then she looked at the pie, then she said, 'Give this note back when you go'. I did. And, sure enough, I got whipped with the bullocks cane again.

Nell was a cruel woman, she had a hard heart. When she wasn't whippin' us girls with the bullocks cane for not workin' hard enough, she was hittin' us over the head.

---

homestead: farmhouse in Australia
tucker: Australian word for food

She didn't like natives. If one of us was in her way and we didn't move real quick, she'd give us a real hard thump over the head, just like that. Ooh, it hurt! White people are great ones for thumpin' you on the head, aren't they? We was only kids.

Aah, but they were good old days, then. I never seen days like that ever again. When they took me from the station, I never seen days like that ever again.

They told my mother I was goin' to get educated. They told all the people I was goin' to school. I thought it'd be good, goin' to school. I thought I'd be somebody real important. My mother wanted me to learn to read and write like white people. Then she wanted me to come back and teach her. There was a lot of the older people interested in learnin' how to read and write, then.

Why did they tell my mother that lie? Why do white people tell so many lies? I got nothin' out of their promises. My mother wouldn't have let me go just to work. God will make them pay for their lies. He's got people like that under the whip. They should have told my mother the truth. She thought I was coming back.

When I left, I was cryin', all the people were cryin', my mother was cryin' and beatin' her head. Lily was cryin'. I called, 'Mum, Mum, Mum!' She said, 'Don't forget me, Talahue!'

They all thought I was coming back. I thought I'd only be gone a little while. I could hear their wailing for miles and miles. 'Talahue! Talahue!' They were singin' out my name, over and over. I couldn't stop cryin'. I kept callin', 'Mum! Mum!'

Daisy was not, in fact, going away to be educated. Although she did not know it, she was taken to the city of Perth to work as a servant in a white Australian's house.

Bound feet
Jung Chang

Jung Chang's book Wild Swans *is an amazing story of life in China during the twentieth century. For a long time, China had little contact with the rest of the world and ancient customs and traditions were preserved without change for many centuries. One of these customs – binding the feet of baby girls – was still being followed in the early years of the twentieth century: small feet were thought to be a sign of beauty. Jung Chang's grandmother was one of the last to suffer this ordeal.*

My grandmother's feet had been bound when she was two years old. Her mother, who herself had bound feet, first wound a piece of white cloth about twenty feet long round her feet, bending all the toes except the big toe inward and under the sole. Then she placed a large stone on top to crush the arch. My grandmother screamed in agony and begged her to stop. Her mother had to stick a cloth into her mouth to gag her. My grandmother passed out repeatedly from the pain.

The process lasted several years. Even after the bones had been broken, the feet had to be bound day and night in thick cloth because the moment they were released they would try to recover. For years my grandmother lived in relentless, **excruciating** pain. When she pleaded with her mother to untie the bindings, her mother would weep and tell her that unbound feet would ruin her entire life, and that she was doing it for her own future happiness.

---

excruciating: extremely painful

In those days, when a woman was married, the first thing the bridegroom's family did was to examine her feet. Large feet, meaning normal feet, were considered to bring shame on the husband's household. The mother-in-law would lift the hem of the bride's long skirt, and if the feet were more than about four inches long, she would throw down the skirt **in a demonstrative gesture of contempt** and stalk off, leaving the bride to the critical gaze of the wedding guests, who would stare at her feet and insultingly mutter their **disdain**. Sometimes a mother would take pity on her daughter and remove the binding cloth; but when the child grew up and had to endure the contempt of her husband's family and the disapproval of society, she would blame her mother for having been too weak.

The practice of binding feet was originally introduced about a thousand years ago, **allegedly** by a **concubine** of the emperor. Not only was the sight of women hobbling on tiny feet considered **erotic**, men would also get excited playing with bound feet, which were always hidden in embroidered silk shoes. Women could not remove the binding cloths even when they were adults, as their feet would start growing again. The binding could only be loosened temporarily at night in bed, when they would put on soft-soled shoes. Men rarely saw naked bound feet, which were usually covered in rotting flesh and stank when the bindings were removed. As a child, I can remember my grandmother being in constant pain. When we came home from shopping, the first thing she

---

excruciating: extremely painful

in a demonstrative gesture of contempt: dramatically showing how much she despised the unshortened feet

disdain: scorn, contempt

allegedly: it is said; supposedly

concubine: a partner of the emperor's who is not his wife

erotic: sexually exciting

would do was soak her feet in a bowl of hot water, sighing with relief as she did so. Then she would set about cutting off pieces of dead skin. The pain came not only from the broken bones, but also from her toenails, which grew into the balls of her feet.

In fact, my grandmother's feet were bound just at the moment when foot-binding was disappearing for good. By the time her sister was born in 1917, the practice had virtually been abandoned, so she escaped the torment.

A Ghanaian funeral
BBC News Online

Despite the mournful title of this next extract, it is actually a light-hearted and humorous story which shows just how imaginative and inventive people can be. It all happened in Ghana and appeared as a report on BBC News Online.

Ghanaian attends his own funeral

Mourners at a Ghanaian funeral were astounded when the 'dead' man arrived for the ceremony, reports Kweku Sakyi Addo from Accra. There has been drama about life and death in the village of Adaklu-Dabalu in the Volta region of Ghana, with **a moral** about who is more deserving of the family's money – the living or the dead.

It began when Cujoe Gokah, 32, who had had surgery for a **hernia**, could not raise 450 000 cedi (£60) to pay hospital bills. After several fruitless attempts by the hospital to get the family to pool the cash to pay the bill, surgeon Dr A K Tachie came up with a fundraising idea bound to hit the target.

According to the *Ghanaian Times*, the surgeon sent a message to Cujoe's family that he had died. The response was prompt and efficient. The family sent a **delegation** to settle all the medical bills, and arranged for the body to be handed over for the funeral and burial.

---

a moral: a message
hernia: a rupture, in which an internal part of the body pushes through another part
delegation: official representative group

A few days later mourners arrived dressed in red and black, chanting funeral **dirges** and singing the praises of the one they had lost. They had even bought a coffin which they brought along. Suddenly Cujoe appeared in the door, to the astonishment of the mourners. The doctor explained it had been his **ploy** to get them to pay Cujoe's bills.

Their joy at finding Cujoe alive was much stronger than any anger at the doctor's trickery. Their dirges turned to songs of happiness. They covered Cujoe from head to toe in talcum powder, which is a symbol of triumph, and carried him shoulder high. Instead of weeping there was dancing and singing and merrymaking all night when they returned to Cujoe's village. They returned the coffin to the coffin-maker, who graciously took it back and returned their money.

Cujoe has since become a tourist attraction. Schoolchildren are paying **100 cedi** a time to see a man who once – sort of – died, but now lives.

---

dirges: sad songs
ploy: trick or plan
100 cedi: about one-and-a-third pence

Home sweet home
John Peel

To complete this section, radio presenter John Peel writes about the importance that people attach to their home. But, as he explains, different members of the same family can have very different views on what makes home 'home'.

The door into the garden is open. Outside the birds sing, the sun shines, the grass grows. Inside, the **dehumidifiers** hum. We've lived in this place for 29 years now and it looks very different from how it did 29 years ago. Then crops grew (not terribly well) to within **25 feet** of the door and the only trees within view of where I sit at the kitchen table were self-seeded **bullace** along the rim of the ditch that marked the edge of the garden. Now there are trees everywhere. Sheila would tell me what they are, but she's standing in the road talking to Sandy, our neighbour. And there are shrubs and loads of grass. No decking, though, no water features – no pop, no style, we

---

dehumidifiers: devices to reduce moisture in the air
25 feet: 8 metres
bullace: wild plum-tree

strikkly roots and shoots. With a bit of outside help, we just about **keep abreast of** the work needed to maintain the house and garden, but that won't always be the case. Eventually, I suppose, we'll have to sell our home and move to somewhere smaller, more manageable and perhaps nearer to the sea. (Although, if recent grim predictions about global warming are correct, we could stay here and the sea will come to us eventually.)

When my parents divorced I was about 16, and I think I regretted the loss of our home in Cheshire more than I regretted the divorce. People came and went, as they do, throughout our childhood, but the house was a constant and you learnt to play upon it as upon a stringed instrument. We valued not just the openness and the coolness but the darker corners, the skirting boards, the suspicion of damp, the infinite strangeness of the kitchen range. My brothers and I still **detour** past the house when we're in the area, although it looks less and less like our old home each time we do. Our children will presumably feel the same about this house. Indeed, they already do, and we are used to being told off for making changes that, in our Tom's words, destroy their childhood. There was an unsightly mound of grassed-over builder's rubble, for example, on which grass never really grew and the trees we planted died. Eventually we had it cleared away, only to be told that what was, to us, a mess was, to the children, as fine a feature as any garden could boast. Then there was the old wooden container that served as a den. This grew mouldy and rotten and too small for growing children before we broke it up and disposed of it. Vital, it transpired later. But the house remains pretty much as it

---

strikkly: strictly
keep abreast of: manage to do
detour: go a long way around

was – although we did have the upstairs bathroom redone recently. Although three of four children now work or study away, their rooms are still their rooms and I'm seldom happier than when they come back to reoccupy them, however briefly.

Activities

Death of an elephant

1 In this extract, Kuki Gallman retells an experience she had in Africa watching a friend kill an elephant. A piece of writing like this is called a recount text because the writer is recounting (or retelling) an event. The author structures the text by first setting the scene, then recounting events as they happen, and ending with a significant closing statement. Find examples of each of these structural features and try to describe their effect on the reader.

2 Kuki Gallman manages to convey what a terrible waste it was to kill such a magnificent and harmless animal. When she approaches the creature's eye, she finds that it acts like a mirror in which she can see herself. In pairs, talk about what this made her feel. For example:

- why does she stress that she saw 'a smaller image of myself' and 'felt even smaller'?
- what makes her particularly ashamed and shocked?
- what do you think she is going to say in the unfinished question which begins 'What right…'?

3 Write Paolo's diary entry for that day. Say:

- how he killed the elephant
- why he had to kill it
- what he felt after he had killed it
- what he believed Kuki had felt about the killing.

My place

4 Daisy herself could not write: her account was actually written by Sally Morgan. But Sally manages to let you hear Daisy's own voice, by representing the way she speaks. For example, she uses abbreviations, such as 'if I had've known' and 'I 'member once'. She also writes in Daisy's own dialect. A dialect is a variety of the language used by a group of people; it has its own words and

expressions, as well as its own rules of grammar. Write down the standard English version of these words and phrases from Daisy's dialect:

a it was real cold
b that was good tucker
c We was only kids
d I never seen days like that ever again
e I thought I'd be somebody real important.

5 Although Daisy did eat some of the pie, she feels that the punishment was unfair and cruel. Write an account like Daisy's of a moment from your childhood when you were punished unfairly for something. For example, there might have been a moment when you were wrongly blamed for doing something. If you can't think of something that happened to you personally, write about an incident from a book or film.

Bound feet

6 Verbs (words in the sentence which enable us to say what people are doing, or being) are especially important in the first paragraph of the extract, where they help you to understand what happened when a child had her feet bound. In pairs, use these verbs to retell what happened in your own words:

- wound • bending • placed • crush • screamed
- begged • gag • passed out

7 Think about the period that you are studying in your history lessons at the moment. Pick a custom or activity from that period which no longer happens today. Write an account from the point of view of someone involved in the activity, bringing out how cruel or strange it is. (For example, you could write from the point of view of a Roman watching people in the arena fighting to the death, or a witness at a witchcraft trial.) As you write, think about the way in which Jung Chang has used verbs to tell her story clearly and vividly.

A Ghanaian funeral

8 This is a news report from Ghana. It concerns a trick that was played by a doctor in Ghana when a family refused to pay a hospital bill. Typically, the report answers the questions Who, What, Where, How and Why. Read through the report and write a sentence in answer to each question.

9 Write an account of the funeral from the point of view of one of the mourners. Begin by explaining how sad you had been, and then express your joy and amazement at Cujoe's 'return from the dead'. How do you feel about it, looking back? Are you amused, or a little angry at being fooled?

Home sweet home

10 John Peel uses a mixture of the present tense, to show what the home is like now ('The door into the garden is open'), the past tense, to let us know about things that happened earlier ('... I was about 16 ...'), and the future tense, when he is thinking about what might happen one day in the future (' ... we'll have to sell ...').

Copy out the table below. Underline the verb in each quotation. Say which tense it is in.

Quotation	Tense
it <u>looks</u> very different	Present
crops grew (not terribly well) to within 25 feet of the door	
there are trees everywhere	
we just about keep abreast of the work	
that won't always be the case	
the sea will come to us eventually	
I regretted the loss of our home in Cheshire	
My brothers and I still detour past the house	
Our children will presumably feel the same	
Indeed, they already do	
Eventually we had it cleared away	

11 Write about your own home, or one you have read about in a novel or short story. Use the present tense to describe what it is like now, the past tense when you are looking back and the future tense when you are thinking about what might lie ahead.

Comparing the extracts

12 There are very different ways in which someone can write about 'people and places'. In pairs, talk about the differences between these extracts. Give your responses to the following questions:

a Which of these writers (there might be more than one):

- seemed to be looking back with sadness to the place they are describing?
- was taking a light-hearted view of the place, its people and its customs?
- did not approve of the customs they describe?
- was thinking about the present and the future, as well as the past?

b Look back at the extracts and talk about the way they show that:

- people's behaviour is influenced by things that happen to them while they grow up
- people's behaviour is influenced by the customs of the society in which they live.

13 Write a short account of an incident set in a place that you know. Show how the people involved behaved as they did because of their childhood experiences or because of the culture in which they live.

Section 2
Mind your language

The English language is spoken not just in the British Isles but by millions of people around the world. It is no surprise that people sometimes get it wrong. This section is about the many and various ways in which English can be mangled – intentionally or unintentionally.

The mother tongue
Bill Bryson

As an American who lived for a long time in Britain, Bill Bryson became fascinated by the English language – and not just the differences between the ways in which the Americans and the British speak it. This extract is the opening of his book on the English language called The Mother Tongue.

More than 300 million people in the world speak English and the rest, it sometimes seems, try to. It would be **charitable** to say that the results are sometimes mixed.

Consider this hearty announcement in a Yugoslavian hotel: 'The flattening of underwear with pleasure is the job of the chambermaid. Turn to her straightaway.' Or this warning to motorists in Tokyo: 'When a passenger of the foot heave in sight, tootle the horn. Trumpet at him **melodiously** at first, but if he still obstacles your passage,

---

charitable: kind and generous
melodiously: tunefully

then tootle him with vigor.' Or these instructions gracing a packet of convenience food from Italy: '**Besmear** a backing pan, previously buttered with a good tomato sauce, and, after, dispose the cannelloni, lightly distanced between them in a only couch.'

Clearly the writer of *that* message was not about to let a little ignorance of English stand in the way of a good meal. In fact, it would appear that one of the beauties of the English language is that with even the most **tenuous** grasp you can speak volumes if you show enough enthusiasm – a willingness to tootle with vigor, as it were.

To be fair, English is full of booby traps for the **unwary** foreigner. Any language where the **unassuming** word *fly* signifies an annoying insect, a means of travel, and a critical part of a gentleman's **apparel** is clearly asking to be mangled. Imagine being a foreigner and having to learn that in English one tells *a* lie but *the* truth, that a person who says 'I could care less' means the same thing as someone who says 'I couldn't care less,' that a sign in a store saying ALL ITEMS NOT ON SALE doesn't mean literally what it says (that every item is *not* on sale) but rather that only some of the items are on sale, that when a person says to you, 'How do you do?' he will be taken aback if you reply, with **impeccable** logic, 'How do I do what?'

Besmear: spread
tenuous: shaky
unwary: unprepared
unassuming: modest; not making any great claims for itself
apparel: clothes
impeccable: faultless; perfect

Spoken misprints

Have you ever been responsible for an embarrassing misprint, or said something that simply came out wrong? The language expert David Crystal has put together two small collections of mistakes in this article from his Encyclopedia of the English Language. *The first is from a magazine called* Punch; *the second from sports commentaries heard on television and radio.*

MISPRINTS

Humour can arise from an unintentional use of language, resulting in such effects as howlers, misprints, slips of the tongue, and accidental **puns**.

One of the most popular columns in *Punch* magazine was 'Country Life', a readers' selection of the unintentionally humorous in print – misprints, howlers, and bizarre observations sent in from all over the world.

- At one time he was well up in the first ten places, but hitting a bride in Wales damaged the suspension and he dropped back. (*Autosport*)

- Volunteers urgently needed to help stroke patients with speech problems. (*Chorlton and Wilbrampton News*)

- Cross-examined by Mr Quinn, witness said that someone called her husband 'an Irish pig'. She said he was not Irish. (*Biddulph Chronicle*)

- A fifteen-year-old Croydon boy has been suspended by his head since last September because of his long hair. (*Times Educational Supplement*)

puns: jokes that depend on a word having two meanings

- He said it is unlikely pollution is the cause and the fish bore no outwards signs of disease – 'these fish are perfectly healthy, except that they're dead'. (*Vancouver Sun*)

In the British satirical magazine *Private Eye*, there is a column reporting the linguistic howlers made by presenters on radio and television. Most listeners or viewers would probably not have noticed them at the time they were said: the humour lies in seeing them in the cold light of day, and out of context.

- Oh and that's a brilliant shot. The odd thing is his mum's not very keen on snooker.

- Lillian's great strength is her strength.

- Hurricane Higgins can either win or lose this final match tomorrow.

- He and his colleagues are like hungry hounds, galloping after a red herring.

- Only one word for that – magic darts!

- The audience are literally electrified and glued to their seats. (From P. Simpson, 1992)

Here are some more examples of 'spoken misprints' or 'howlers', as David Crystal calls them. The first selection is from the enthusiastic Formula 1 racing commentator

Murray Walker, a man about whom Clive James said: 'In his quieter moments, it sounds as though his trousers are on fire.'

- With half the race gone, there is half the race still to go.
- Do my eyes deceive me, or is Senna's Lotus sounding rough?
- Anything happens in Grand Prix racing and it usually does.
- As you look at the first four, the significant thing is that Alboreto is fifth.
- …Cruel luck for Alesi, second on the grid. That's the first time he had started from the front row in a Grand Prix, having done so in Canada earlier this year…
- This is an interesting circuit because it has **inclines**, and not just up, but down as well.
- And the first five places are filled by five different cars.
- Tambay's hopes, which were nil before, are absolutely zero now.
- Alain Prost is in a commanding second place.
- He's watching us from hospital with his injured knee.
- Mansell is slowing it down, taking it easy. Oh no he isn't! It's a lap record.
- Schumacher has made his final stop three times!
- I know it's an old **cliché**, but you can cut the atmosphere with a cricket stump.
- Into lap 53, the **penultimate** last lap but one.
- And Panis is almost literally laughing his head off in that car.

inclines: slopes
cliché: a saying that is used too often
penultimate: last but one

- If I was Michael Schumacher . . . which of course I am not . . .
- Well, he's world champion, and we only get one of those a year.
- I should imagine that the conditions in the cockpit are unimaginable!
- I can't believe what's happening visually, in front of my eyes.
- That's history. I say history because it happened in the past.

Although Murray Walker is the unchallenged expert, mistakes of this kind have come to be known as 'Colemanballs', after the sports commentator David Coleman. Here are some more examples from a variety of television news reporters and figures from the world of sport.

- If England are going to win this match, they're going to have to score a goal. (*Jimmy Hill, BBC*)

- He's a guy who gets up at six o'clock in the morning regardless of what time it is. (*Lou Duva, veteran boxing trainer, on the training regime of heavyweight Andrew Golota*)

- I would not say David Ginola is the best left-winger in the Premiership, but there are none better. (*Ron Atkinson*)

- He dribbles a lot and the opposition don't like it – you can see it all over their faces. (*Ron Atkinson*)

- I couldn't settle in Italy – it was like living in a foreign country. (*Ian Rush*)

- Street hockey is great for kids. It's energetic, competitive, and skilful. And best of all it keeps them off the street. (*Radio 1 Newsbeat*)

- A fascinating duel between three men . . . (*David Coleman*)
- Ian Mackie is here to prove his back injury is behind him. (*Commentator at Spar Athletics*)
- Apart from their goals, Norway haven't scored. (*Terry Venables*)
- Chile have three options – they could win or they could lose. (*Kevin Keegan*)
- I came to Nantes two years ago and it's much the same today, except that it's completely different. (*Kevin Keegan*)
- They've picked their heads up off the ground and they now have a lot to carry on their shoulders. (*Ron Atkinson*)

- Well, either side could win it, or it could be a draw. (*Ron Atkinson*)
- It's now 1–1, an exact reversal of the score on Saturday. (*Kevin Keegan*)
- Gary always weighed up his options, especially when he had no choice. (*Kevin Keegan, Radio 5 Live*)
- We threw our dice into the ring and turned up trumps. (*Bruce Rioch, ITV*)

A small misunderstanding
Reginald Antony Hutton

Children very often misunderstand what they have been told. Here Reginald Antony Hutton recalls the story of a little English girl living for a while in Khartoum in the Sudan, in north Africa, where her parents were serving in the forces. To get the best out of this story it helps to know that General Gordon had led the British army in a war in the Sudan in the nineteenth century and was a very famous soldier.

In Khartoum in the garden of Gordon College stands an imposing statue of General Gordon mounted on a camel. General Gordon is in full dress with plumed helmet, medals, sword, boots and spurs. His camel, a magnificent Sudanese beast, is gaily dressed in rugs with bells and tassels.

A small English girl who lived not far away used to love going to the college garden and playing near the Gordon statue. In fact she became so attached to it that she never seemed happier than when it was close at hand.

At last the time came when her father was transferred from Khartoum and her mother took the little girl to the college garden for the last time to say 'goodbye' to her beloved Gordon. There she stood enthralled, full of respect and admiration. Her mother eventually led her away, and walking slowly down the garden path the girl constantly whispered:

'Goodbye Gordon, goodbye Gordon, goodbye Gordon.'

A short way down the road the little girl turned to her mother and said:

'Tell me, mummy – I've always wanted to know – who is the funny little man on Gordon?'

Playing with words
Simon Elmes

There seems to be something about English words that makes people want to play with them. Think about the many jokes which depend on word-play, such as puns and double-meanings; or the way writers give their characters funny and strange-sounding names. Simon Elmes is the writer of a radio series called The Routes of English *(a title which itself contains a pun). Here he talks about the fun that can be had with words.*

What makes a good joke? Is it the situation? Or maybe the **punchline**? Or is it the knock-em over, falling-about-pleasures of good slapstick? The chances are that whatever the humour is, unless we are talking about mime artists like Marcel Marceau or the great Jacques Tati, there are going to be words in it somewhere. They are at the very heart of what makes us laugh. What has made the English split their sides over the centuries has been the comedy of words.

This is Ronnie Barker, one of the most popular comedians of the last fifty years, in serious appeal-to-the-nation mode, looking straight at the camera:

---

punchline: the funny or surprise ending of a joke

I am the secretary for the *Loyal* Society for the Relief of Sufferers from *Pissmonunciation* . . . (big laughs) and the reason I am once more *squeaking* to you tonight . . . (more laughter), is that many people last time couldn't understand what I was *spraying*. So here I am back again on your little *queens* to *strain* it and make it all *queer* for you. (hysterical laughter and applause)

Wit, puns, **spoonerisms**, even inaccurate ones like Ronnie's play-on-words, silly suggestive names, ***double entendres***, **malapropisms**, good word jokes, bad word jokes, the BBC air waves have been filled with the sound of people playing with language. In the final series of Rowan Atkinson's celebrated TV comedy, Blackadder has only to address the hapless Captain Darling, without crediting him with his full title, for the audience to fall about:

Blackadder: What do you want, Darling?
Darling: It's Captain Darling to you . . .

---

spoonerisms: accidentally swapping over the initial letters of two words, like 'par cark'
double entendres: (a French expression) double meanings
malapropisms: words comically confused with others that sound similar, as in, 'We went to Calais by *fairy*', instead of *ferry*

They never tire of the joke. This sort of *double entendre* is as old as language itself. It is one of the many forms of linguistic misunderstanding based on confusing one word with another that sounds the same. Shakespeare was not above making his Frenchmen pronounce the word *third* in habitual manner without the '*h*', and gets a cheap laugh every time. And in *Much Ado About Nothing*, Beatrice calls Count Claudio ' . . . *(as) civil as an orange*' – the sort of pun that would make today's, and I suspect sixteenth-century, audiences groan at its **ludicrous approximation** (*civil* sounding like *Seville*, where the oranges come from). A good contemporary pun, the fruit – and the **neologism** *orange* that was imported with it – arrived on Britain's shores about a hundred or so years before Shakespeare was writing. And there's a little linguistic curiosity here too: a *norange* was originally closer in sound to the *naranja* of Spain, but the word division appears to have shifted over time. It's an example of the way words change, enriching the game of playing with language.

Professor Walter Redfern of the University of Reading, who has written a book about puns, believes that:

Word play is economical: you can say something in a much shorter space and much shorter time by a pun or by some other form of word play than you can if you had to spell it all out.

Homophones (words that sound alike), **homographs** (words that are written alike), alliteration, assonance (the

---

ludicrous approximation: the pun is ridiculous because 'civil' only sounds roughly like 'Seville'

neologism: a newly invented word, like *byte* (in computers)

homophones: words that sound the same but have different meanings, like *two* and *too*

homographs: words that are spelled the same but have different meanings, like the *bark* of a tree and the *bark* of a dog

repetition of sounds) and rhyme all come to the aid of the punster, the man or woman who likes to play with words. And, ultimately, that is what we are talking about when we refer to verbal jokes. It's all language play, the cut and thrust of meaning and **morphology**, of word-shape and word-sound. For most of us it is completely without material purpose, so why do so many of us do it?

According to Professor David Crystal, author of many authoritative works on language and compiler of the *Cambridge Encyclopedia of the English Language*, people play with language for a whole range of different reasons. Some do it because they simply want a good laugh and the play of the moment gives them that possibility. Other people play with words because they are fascinated with language and want to explore its potential for variation and creativity. Yet others do it because they feel competitive and want to beat somebody at this business of getting to grips with language and being in control over it.

There are all sorts of different reasons. I suppose the bottom line is that people play with language because it's there, and whenever you're faced with something as intricate and complex and as fascinating as language, you want to get the most out of it.

Playing with words is a natural human activity, from the first babblings of a child taking his or her first steps in language, to the normal to and fro of conversation at the dinner table. David Crystal recalls one such moment:

One of the occasions I remember very well was when somebody referred to their cat meeting a neighbour's cat in the middle of the road. And, quick as a flash, one of the people in the group said, 'Oh there was a cat-frontation', obviously based on 'confrontation'. Now that might have been left there, but it wasn't. The other

---

morphology: the study of the form of words

people in the group started to chip in. One of them said, 'Oh that was a cat-astrophe', and then someone else said, 'Oh that was a cat-alyst for further meetings', and somebody else said, 'Oh but one of the cats wasn't very well: she had cat-arrh'.

And so the joke went bouncing around until people got fed up with it or simply ran out of words beginning with 'cat'. At that point, the conversation goes back onto an even keel until someone else makes another comment which generates another pun and the cycle goes round again.

This sort of 'ping-pong punning', as it is sometimes known, is a familiar human phenomenon, amongst people who have only just met almost as much as amongst old friends. People indulge in word play, according to Professor Crystal, as a good way of beginning to knot the bonds of friendship. And the **benchmark** of approval amongst the assembled company is usually not the traditional chortle but a groan; the bigger the groan, the more successful the pun.

---

benchmark: a way of judging how good something is

Activities

The mother tongue

1 In pairs, pick out the two or three main points about the English language that Bill Bryson is making in this introductory passage. Look at, for example, 'More than . . . try to'; 'one of the beauties . . . it were.'; and 'To be fair . . . foreigner.'

2 It is easy to spot mistakes in the English language, but not always so easy to put them right.

  a Try to redraft each of the examples of mistaken English so that it states clearly what the person was trying to say:

  • the flattening of underwear . . .
  • When a passenger . . .
  • Besmear a backing-pan . . .

  b Write three sentences which clearly show the three different meanings of 'fly'.

Spoken misprints

3 A number of the slips in these quotations can be placed under certain headings.

  • Some quotations are *non-sequiturs* (in which the second half of a statement simply does not follow from the first. 'Non sequitur' is a Latin phrase which means 'it does not follow'.) An example is: 'Oh and that's a brilliant shot. The odd thing is his mum's not very keen on snooker.'
  • Several other quotes are examples of *tautology* (saying the same thing twice, in different words), for example: 'I can't believe what's happening visually, in front of my eyes.'
  • There are also a number of instances of *stating the obvious*: 'If England are going to win this match, they're going to have to score a goal.'

- Commentators often misuse the word *literally* (which should only be used when the words describe exactly what is happening): 'The audience are literally electrified and glued to their seats.'
- They also use *mixed metaphors* (starting off with one comparison and unintentionally switching to another): 'They've picked their heads up off the ground and they now have a lot to carry on their shoulders'.

Draw a large table with five columns. Write these headings in the first row:

non-sequitur; tautology; stating the obvious; misusing 'literally'; mixed metaphors

Find further examples of these five kinds of mistakes from pages 23–26. List each one under the correct heading.

4 In pairs, talk about your favourite examples from the list and explain why you like them. You might be able to add other examples that you have heard on television or radio.

A small misunderstanding

5 This kind of story is called an *anecdote*; it is short, amusing, and about a real person or incident. Anecdotes, like jokes, often have a punchline (a surprise, comic ending), and this one is in the form of some dialogue between the child and her mother. Talk in pairs about the clever way in which the narrator manages to achieve a surprise ending. For example, what important information does he hold back from the reader?

6 Write an anecdote of your own. Remember that an anecdote should be:

- fairly short (this one is under 200 words)
- amusing (think about the possibility of a punchline)
- about a real person or incident.

You could relate something that happened at school, for example, or when you were much younger.

Playing with words

7 There are a number of technical terms to do with language used in the extract, including:

homophone, malapropism, homograph, pun, neologism, double entendre, spoonerism.

a In pairs, make a table like the one below. Write the technical term in the first column.

b In the second column, write the definition. If you do not already know it, you can find it in one of the footnotes.

c In the third column, write an example from the extract or a footnote. Then add two more examples of your own.

Technical term	Definition	Example

Comparing the extracts

8 In pairs, look back through the extracts and their activities and talk about each of the following terms or phrases, to make sure you know what it means:

howler, non-sequitur, tautology, stating the obvious, misusing 'literally', mixed metaphors, anecdote, punchline, pun, spoonerism, double entendre, malapropism, neologism, homophone, homograph.

9 What things about the English language make you laugh? Use the ideas and information in the extracts to write a short article on what Simon Elmes calls 'the comedy of words'. You will need to write about some of the features you have just been discussing and quote your favourite examples. You could also include some quotes from stand-up comics who play with language, such as Ant and Dec.

Section 3
Other times

It is difficult to put ourselves into the shoes of people who lived in other centuries – or even only a few years back. This section contains records of the very different lives that people led at various times from the 1820s to the 1950s. They show that, although times have changed, people remain essentially the same.

Rabbiting
Joe Ackerley

This first extract comes from the middle of the twentieth century. But the experience it describes could have happened at any time since people first hunted and killed animals.

Victor and I took little Bernard, aged ten?, for a walk rabbiting. He is the son of an **embezzler**, serving some years in prison, a curious child with enormous blue eyes, rather uncanny. He begged to be taken. He was in warlike **attire** – Indian trousers made of sacking, gum boots and a metal rod which he said was a gun. We had not gone far when Tripp, the hotel dog, **located** a rabbit in a bramble clump and killed it. He took some time to kill it, owing to

---

embezzler: someone who dishonestly takes money that has been left in their care
attire: clothes, outfit
located: found

the thickness of the undergrowth in which they both were, so that he could not get at the rabbit properly. He is said not to be good at killing things anyway. Quick though he is to catch them. So the rabbit squealed and squealed.

The effect on Bernard was most interesting. He almost had **hysterics**. He was quite **overwrought**. 'No. No. Oh, look, look. Let me. Let me. There it is. Oh, stop it, stop it' – all that kind of exclamation; he tried to rush into the bush, jumped about, began to cry, pulled himself together, and every now and then looked into my face, gave a sort of smile, and then darted back to the bush again. All within a minute. Victor was very good with him. He commanded him firmly to behave, said he would send him home if he misbehaved, and pulling the still-alive though bleeding rabbit out of the bush, **dispatched** it with a single blow of his hand. Then he told Bernard that he must not be so silly, rabbits were **vermin** and had to be killed and that if he wanted to come hunting he must get used to it. Bernard recovered and wanted and was

---

hysterics: fit of uncontrolled emotional excitement
overwrought: extremely upset
dispatched: killed
vermin: pests

allowed to carry the corpse, but every now and then as we walked he remarked, 'I heard it squeal. I heard it squeal.' Later on, since it was awkward for him to carry it by its legs in his hand, we decided to tie my dog's lead to it so that he could sling it over his shoulder. Before doing this, Victor held the rabbit by its ears and shook it, so that the contents of its bowels and bladder fell out. Then he tied my lead round its legs. He pulled the knot tight. 'Not so tight! Not so tight!' cried poor little Bernard, thinking for a moment still that the rabbit was being hurt. Then he appeared to forget and became a mighty hunter, pretending to shoot more rabbits and birds with his metal rod.

Of course it was disgusting, say what one may about vermin, and *I* disliked it too, but life has **inured me** to its horrors. The episode will obviously be remembered by Bernard all his life. (Though he had wanted to come out hunting rabbits, he has always wanted a pet rabbit for his own.) Whether it will affect his life, and if so for good or ill, who can tell. It was certainly a frightful shock to him.

And vermin! How **arrogant** people are. Does the earth belong to them? Do not the rabbits think *them* vermin too, so to speak. And are they, in fact, not a greater menace to the whole living world than the rabbits themselves?

---

inured me: made me accustomed (to something unpleasant)
arrogant: self-important

Childhood among the bomb-sites
Ray Puxley

Not everybody's memories of war and its aftermath are bad. Ray Puxley grew up in London just after the Second World War had ended and joyfully recalls the opportunities offered by the bomb-sites and damaged buildings.

The fifties was a great time to be a kid, especially in Poplar where I grew up. Being near the docks it was a regular target of the **Luftwaffe** during the **Blitz** and almost every street bore the scars of that one-sided encounter. Vast tracts of rubble-strewn wastelands overgrown with a multitude of weeds and wild flowers. And stinging nettles that I swear used to reach out to deliver their spite to the backs of little bare legs. These were our playgrounds. Each child belonged to a gang and every gang had their 'debry' (debris). Most of the time this was fine, there was no real **animosity** and most of the kids were friends. They played together, members of opposing gangs sat next to each other in school. Then, once a year came the wood war season. This occurred in the week leading up to 5 November, when all gang members would scour the streets for bonfire wood and inter-debry rivalry became intense. Now at that time the neighbourhood had a profusion of bombed houses, therefore there was a plentiful supply of wood and other **combustibles**. But

---

Luftwaffe: German airforce
Blitz: the series of heavy bombing raids on London in 1941–42
animosity: a feeling that you are someone's enemy
combustibles: things that would burn

that wasn't good enough. What we had, they wanted and what they had, we had to have. Raids were mounted into 'enemy territory'. This usually happened between five and six o'clock when your scouts came back and reported that all enemy personnel had gone for their teas. There was always a guard but he didn't count because he was always the youngest in the gang. He would stand resolutely at his post, a saucepan on his head and a stick in his hand and a mind full of valour. But at the first sign of a screaming, club-wielding bunch of urchins charging towards him he'd be off in the opposite direction to raise the alarm. As if **synchronized**, nearby doors would open **in unison** and the opposing army would spill out into the street to begin the battle. Boys would trade blows over a rotted piece of tarpaulin. An old rafter would be the prize in a splintery game of tug o'war. The raiders would eventually retreat taking with them whatever they could. The next night they would be the raided. That's how it was, perfectly good friends would fight each other over a piece of wood that they may have stepped over 365 times since last year.

With no television to keep us in and no traffic to present any danger, the street was everything we needed. It was our football pitch in winter, our cricket pitch in summer (the two seasons never crossed) and our race track. On long summer nights everybody, children and adults, would be out, playing, talking, sometimes arguing until it was dark. Those streets are not there any more, they were pulled down at the end of the sixties to make way for a housing estate. In dreams I often return.

---

synchronized: arranged to happen at the same time
in unison: at the same time

Local hero
Nina Slingsby Smith

George Slingsby and his brother Arthur were servants on a wealthy estate and did not have a bad life. But, when war was declared in 1914, they both decided to join up. George was to find that not everybody was as determined to enlist as he was.

Practically every able-bodied young male on the estate was now in uniform. 'Young Master Jackie' Whitaker had gone to France with his regiment, leaving Arthur feeling like the tail on the donkey. The war that people had said would be over by Christmas was fast approaching its second Christmas as it still raged on in ever-worsening conditions for both men and animals. To add to the misery of existing like rats in mud-filled trenches, often ill-fed and ill-clad, the troops were now also at the mercy of Germany's latest weapon – chlorine gas. As yet, the horrors of mustard gas were still unimagined. George had already experienced enough of the enemy's mercy in war. He had only to close his eyes to see again the rows of dead faces in that small **Queenstown** harbour. Yet the brothers felt impelled to make their contribution to the defeat of people who brought such horrors into the world.

It was easier to make the resolve, however, than to carry it out. Both their employers were desperate at the prospect of losing such vital members of their almost

---

Queenstown: George had been on the *Lusitania* when it was torpedoed with the loss of 1201 lives; the survivors were brought into Queenstown harbour, Ireland

irreplaceable staff. Though Sir Frederick understood George's feelings after all they had been through together, he still maintained that George was doing vital war work already by working for him. Neither George nor Arthur wished to leave their respected **benefactors** high and dry at the start of a very busy season, but both **were adamant** that they would join up together as soon as they could reasonably be spared from present employment. Their parents took the news calmly and, with reluctant resignation, so did Sir Frederick.

George and Arthur desperately wanted to remain together in the army. Had they been able to volunteer together before Christmas 1915 it might have been possible. With the passing of the Military Services Act early in 1916, George was to find that he could no longer enlist where he liked. Instead of the two signing on together in their home town, George found that, owing to his long residence in Enfield, he would be registered in North London. The best that could be arranged was to enlist on the same day and apply for the same regiment.

At Mill Hill, George was received by the recruiting sergeant, given an identity card and sent before a medical board. Apprehensively he entered a large waiting room, where a number of men sat around naked, looking **pensive**. He was told to strip off in one of the cubicles and take his turn with the rest. It came as a shock to a fellow who had always enjoyed his privacy. He was determined to keep his trousers until the very last minute, which caused some **ribald** jokes on the part of the others waiting. Then someone caused a stir by confiding that he had no intention of joining what he

---

benefactors: people who supported them
were adamant: refused to change their minds
pensive: thoughtful
ribald: 'dirty'

called 'their bloody **fiasco**'. He had a friend, he told them, who worked in a hospital and who had given him an **infallible** way of **working his ticket**.

'I've got a decent job and responsibilities at home,' he said. 'They're not getting me to fight their bloody war, not if I can help it.'

They watched him chew his way through half a bar of Sunlight soap which, he explained, produced every symptom of heart disease. He could scarcely have realised he was one of the first conscripts among a gathering largely made up of eager volunteers.

The examination began and they were called in turn to see the doctors. George noticed the soap-eater had suddenly gone very quiet and was looking decidedly under the weather. His **countenance** changed from a flushed pink to deathly white, and finally to a grey-green, before he was finally sick. A doctor came to attend to him and the game was up, for there were enough soap suds on the floor to have done the weekly wash. He was taken into the consulting room at once and emerged after a short time with a strained expression and clutching a card which read 'A.1'.

When George's turn came, he was first handed a list of disorders and told to tick those with which he had been afflicted at any time. George hadn't realised there were so many ailments. When the physical examination began, the ugly lump on his instep was noticed almost at once. He had decided not to mention his recent experience as a passenger on the ill-fated *Lusitania*, in case it **jeopardised** his chances of being accepted; now he was

---

fiasco: shambles
infallible: foolproof; it could not fail
working his ticket: being excused military service
countenance: face
jeopardised: endangered; put at risk

obliged to explain. He answered all their questions and pleaded to be allowed to enter the army, but the examiners were adamant: he would be of no use to the armed forces with an injury of that kind. They graded him C.3, with a recommendation for other work of national importance.

The only person to be pleased by this outcome was Sir Frederick, who considered that George was already engaged in work of national importance, by working for him in his present position. He was convinced that he could get George exempt from what he called '**mundane labour**'.

'It would be such a damned silly waste, George,' he said. 'In the time they take to teach you how to operate the machinery, the war will be over and I shall have lost a good **valet** needlessly.'

George was inclined to agree with him in one respect; nobody could have rated him highly as a handyman. He knew his own profession, but he had never been able to knock a nail in straight. At the moment he was too disappointed to care.

He wrote to his brother, telling him the news. Several days later Arthur replied that he had been accepted for the army. Their plan to be together was not to be fulfilled, and Arthur was sent to France almost immediately after his call-up in the spring of 1916.

In April 1917 news came that George's brother, Arthur, had died in France of pneumonia.

---

mundane labour: unskilled, day-to-day work
valet: a servant who looks after the master's clothes

Factory child
Patrick Rooke

If you had been a child in one of the poorer parts of Britain in the mid-nineteenth century, the chances are that you would have ended up working in a factory. The conditions were dreadful and the supervisors often cruel and violent. This extract includes some of the children's own reports of the harsh treatment they had received. It is taken from a book called The Age of Dickens, *and this chapter is about factory life in the 1830s.*

Thousands of children worked in the factories of Scotland and the North. Very few ever went to school. Although boys and girls were not supposed to start work until they were at least six years old, many began at a younger age. Their hours were long and their tasks **monotonous**. To this hard routine might be added the cruelty of the **overseer**.

The Report of the Commissioners on the employment of children in factories (1833) gives evidence: 'The commissioners have everywhere investigated with the utmost care the treatment to which children are subjected while engaged in the labour of the factory. These inquiries have obtained from the children themselves, from their parents, from **operatives**, overlookers, **proprietors, medical practitioners**, and magistrates, such statements amongst others as the following:

monotonous: unchanging; repetitive and boring
overseer: person who supervised the children
operatives: machine-workers
proprietors: factory owners
medical practitioners: doctors

'When she was a child too little to put on her ain claithes the overlooker used to beat her till she screamed again.'

'Gets many a good beating and swearing. They are all very ill used. The overseer carries a strap.'

'Has been licked four or five times.'

'The boys are often severely strapped; the girls sometimes get a clout. The mothers often complain of this. Has seen the boys have black and blue marks after strapping.'

'Three weeks ago the overseer struck him in the eye with his clenched fist so as to force him to be absent two days; another overseer used to beat him with his fist, striking him so that his arm was black and blue.'

'Has often seen the workers beat cruelly. Has seen the girls strapped; but the boys were beat so that they fell to the floor in the course of the beating, with a rope with four tails, called a cat. Has seen the boys black and blue, crying for mercy.'

Struck with a guilty conscience, Joseph Badder, a spinner, also gave evidence to the Commissioners: 'I have frequently had complaints against myself by the parents of children for beating them. I used to beat them. I am sure that no man can do without it who works long hours; I am sure he cannot. I told them I was very sorry

after I had done it, but I was forced to it. The master expected me to do my work, and I could not do mine unless they did theirs . . .

'I have seen them fall asleep, and they have been performing their work with their hands while they were asleep, after the **billy** had stopped, when their work was over. I have stopped and looked at them for two minutes, going through the motions of **piecening** fast asleep, when there was really no work to do, and they were really doing nothing.'

---

billy: machine (in this case, for spinning)
piecening: joining broken threads (one of the jobs the children performed)

Cheating a dying man
William Cobbett

William Cobbett was a Hampshire farmer's son, born in 1763. With no real schooling, Cobbett educated himself, became a well-known political writer, and ended up as Member of Parliament for Oldham. This account of a visit to a dying friend, the Baron, is typical of Cobbett's 'plain, broad, downright English', as one fellow-writer called it.

Before the summer of 1822, I had not seen him for a year or two, perhaps. But, in July of that year, on a very hot day, I was going down Rathbone Place, and, happening to cast my eye on the Baron's house, I knocked at the door to ask how he was. His man servant came to the door, and told me that his master was at dinner. 'Well,' said I, 'never mind; give my best respects to him.' But, the servant (who had always been with him since I knew him) begged me to come in, for that he was sure his master would be glad to see me. I thought, as it was likely that I might never see him again, I would go in. The servant announced me, and the Baron said, 'Beg him to walk in.' In I went, and there I found the Baron at dinner; but not quite alone; nor without **spiritual** as well as **carnal and vegetable nourishment** before him: for, there, on the opposite side of his ***vis-à-vis* dining table**, sat that nice, neat, straight, prim **piece of mortality**, commonly called

---

spiritual ... nourishment: 'food' for his soul
carnal ... nourishment: meat and vegetables
***vis-à-vis* dining table**: one at which people sit opposite each other
piece of mortality: human being

the Reverend Robert Fellowes, who was now, I could clearly see, **in a fair way enough**. I had dined, and so I let them dine on. The Baron was become quite a child, or worse, as to mind, though he ate as heartily as I ever saw him, and he was always a great eater. When his servant said, 'Here is Mr Cobbett, Sir;' he said, 'How do you do, Sir? I have read much of your writings, Sir; but never had the pleasure to see your person before.' After a time I made him **recollect me**; but, he, directly after, being about to relate something about America, turned towards me, and said, 'Were you ever **in America, Sir?**'

At the end of about half an hour, or, it might be more, I shook hands with the poor old Baron for the last time, well convinced that I should never see him again, and not less convinced, that I had seen his **heir**. He died in about a year or so afterwards, left to his own family about £20 000, and to his **ghostly** guide, the Holy Robert Fellowes, all the rest of his immense fortune, which, as I have been told, amounts to more than a quarter of a million of money.

I see this poor, foolish old man leaving a monstrous mass of money to this little Protestant parson, whom he had not even known more, I believe, than about three or four years. When the will was made I cannot say. I know nothing at all about that. I am supposing that all was perfectly fair; that the Baron had his senses when he made his will; that he clearly meant to do that which he did. But, then, I must insist, that, if he had left the money to a Catholic priest, to

---

in a fair way enough: well-off; doing very well for himself
recollect me: remember who I was
'. . . **in America, Sir?**': It was well known that Cobbett had spent a long time in America and had written a great deal about it; but the Baron's memory was failing
heir: someone who will inherit all the Baron's money
ghostly: spiritual; religious

be by him **expended** on the **endowment** of a convent, wherein to say masses and to feed and teach the poor, it would have been a more sensible and public-spirited part in the Baron, much more beneficial to the town and **environs** of Reigate, and beyond all measure more honourable to his own memory.

---

expended: spent
endowment: providing money to set something up
environs: surrounding area

Activities

Rabbiting

1 This account has an interesting structure. It is divided into four paragraphs. The first paragraph sets the scene and ends with the rabbit being killed. The long second paragraph is about the effect on Bernard and what Victor said to him.

a What is the third paragraph about? And what new topic does the writer raise in the concluding fourth paragraph?

b Summarise each of the paragraphs in a single sentence. For example, the first one could be: 'Joe and Victor take Bernard out rabbiting and Tripp kills a rabbit.'

2 What do you think Bernard would remember about the incident when he was older? What would he feel? Imagine you are Bernard, and that you are writing your autobiography. Describe this incident from Bernard's point of view, explaining how it affected him. Remember to use the first person.

Childhood among the bomb-sites

3 The language used in this account is very colloquial (informal) in style, for example 'great time to be a kid', 'And stinging nettles that I swear . . .' and 'when your scouts came back.' Try to find other examples of this colloquial style. Why do think the writer chose to write his account this way?

4 Think back to when you were younger and a particular incident that you remember. Write an account of what happened. Try to use a similar informal style like Ray Puxley to give it realism.

Local hero

5 An adverb is a word which gives us more information about a verb (or occasionally about an adjective, or another adverb). For example, in the sentence 'The war that people said would be over by Christmas was fast approaching its second Christmas ...', the adverb 'fast' tells us more about the verb 'was ... approaching'.

It is quite possible to produce vivid and exciting descriptions without using adjectives or adverbs. In this extract, however, adverbs have an important part to play. Find the following adverbs and write down the verbs about which they give us more information:

desperately; Apprehensively; decidedly; needlessly; immediately.

6 The account of George Slingsby is written by his oldest daughter, Nina Slingsby Smith. How might George have described the events himself? Write an entry in George's diary for the day of his army medical. Bring out the humour of his experience at the medical (his reluctance to remove his trousers and his amazement at the soap-eater). Remember to use the first person, and that George can say what he thinks and feels about the events.

Factory child

7 In the opening paragraph of this account the writer juxtaposes (puts side by side) opposite ideas about poor children in nineteenth-century Britain. For example, `thousands worked` is contrasted with `few went to school`, and `not supposed to . . . until . . . at least six years old` is juxtaposed with `many began at a younger age. ` What is the effect of using this technique at the start of the piece?

8 In pairs, note down the examples of the cruel treatment suffered by the factory children.

   a In your opinion, which of the statements made at the enquiry is most effective in conveying the harsh conditions in which the children worked?

   b What excuse does Joseph Badder give for beating the

children? Discuss whether it is possible to have any
sympathy with him.

9 People like the famous writer Charles Dickens argued
fiercely against this kind of cruelty in their novels and in
magazines. Write an article for a newspaper or magazine
of the time with the aim of making people aware of the
dreadful conditions endured by children working in
factories. Give your article a striking headline and include
statements from some of the people quoted in the extract.

Cheating a dying man

10 Throughout this piece the writer uses irony (opposite
meaning) and understatement (playing down) to
communicate what he really thinks about how his friend
the Baron disposes of his wealth. For example, when he
says `I am supposing that all was perfectly fair`, he really
means that the Baron was cheated. Find evidence in the
extract to show that Cobbett:

- did not like Fellowes
- could see that he was already quite wealthy, when he
  met him at the Baron's
- knew, when he left the Baron for the last time, that
  Fellowes would inherit his money
- thought it extraordinary that the Baron should leave his
  wealth to someone he had not known very long
- thought that there probably was something suspicious
  about the will
- felt strongly that the Baron could have left his money to
  a worthier cause.

11 How would Fellowes have recalled the meeting with
Cobbett? Write Fellowes's diary entry for that day, in
which he recalls Cobbett's arrival at the Baron's, senses
that Cobbett is suspicious, but thinks over what he is
going to do to get his hands on the Baron's money.

Comparing the extracts

12 When people write about the past, they write with a particular purpose – or variety of purposes – in mind. For example, some are attempting to entertain their readers, while others might want to educate them. In pairs, complete the table below. Say what you think the main purposes of each extract was (you might find two or more main purposes in some of them). The main purposes might have been:

- to help the reader picture a scene or event
- to entertain the reader
- to give information
- to make the reader understand that life was very different in those days
- to express an opinion
- to do something else – if so, say what.

Extract	Main purpose(s)
Rabbiting	

13 Write a short piece about life in a time in the past. You may be able to talk to an older person and use their recollections to write something that is both real and interesting. Otherwise, do some research in history books and encyclopedias or on the Internet.

Think about the different possible approaches that you could take. You could:

- write about the way in which an experience affected somebody (as in *Rabbiting*)
- look back with pleasure to a time which was tough but enjoyable (as in *Childhood among the bomb-sites*)
- describe a very important period in someone's life (as in *Local hero*)
- use facts and quotes to give the reader information (as in *Factory child*)
- relate a single incident and what followed from it (as in *Cheating a dying man*).

Living dangerously

There are a lot of people who cannot bear the thought of a calm, peaceful life with no challenges. In this section you will encounter rattlesnake-chasers, free-fallers, explorers, mountaineers and a round-the-world runner. They make a strange collection, but they all have one thing in common: their love of living dangerously.

Snakes and nutters
From the Independent on Sunday

Many people have a phobia about snakes, but not the residents of Sweetwater. For four days each year, the small Texan town hosts the world's largest rattlesnake round-up, a festival that attracts more than 30 000 visitors. Their prey? The western diamond-back – docile unless provoked, but deadly. Their aim? To harvest as much snake-meat as even the hungriest cowboy can eat...

Rattlesnake venom has a curious effect on the human body, more science fiction than science. First the victim's skin swells to up to three times its normal size. Then the poison – known technically as a haemotoxin – turns everything it comes into contact with into a black mush, as each heartbeat pushes it further into the tissue. The pain is intense. According to Bill Ransberger, a veteran of 42 such bites: 'After 48 hours, maybe the third day, you'll start vomiting. Throughout this time the pain is tremendous because the venom is constantly eating away at your body. Then, after about seven days, the process will either reverse itself or kill you. But, by then, you should have got yourself to a doctor.'

Yet that does not stop hundreds of snake-handlers and snake-hunters – among more than 30 000 visitors – descending on the small Texas town of Sweetwater (population 12 000) for four days each year. There they risk a fatal fang-lashing to participate in the annual 'Rattlesnake Round-up'.

It is not a good time to be a serpent in this part of America's South. Conceived in 1958 by a group of farmers (Ransberger among them) who were fed up with seeing their horses and cattle struck by rattlers, the Sweetwater Round-up is equal parts country fair and animal **lynching**.

Nearly three tons of snakes are 'harvested' each year, brought to the town to be made into belts, handbags, key-rings, walking sticks and boots, not to mention a snakehead in a jar of alcohol – yours for only $10. They are milked for their venom (which is commonly used to treat strokes) and taunted by cowboy-hatted daredevils carrying tongs. In many cases their final fate is to be devoured. Sweetwater's snake-eating contest is a highlight of the festival. And, indeed, with so many hungry people descending on this otherwise quiet town, it is just as well that there is so much cheap snake-meat around.

But first, to misquote the Victorian **culinary** expert Mrs Beeton, you have to catch your snake. The snake-hunters are not all country folk. City slickers and wannabe cowboys seeking a bit of **redneck** excitement pay $60 a time to hunt western diamond-backs on local ranches.

---

lynching: killing without trial
culinary: to do with cookery
redneck: from the southern states of America

Having signed legal **disclaimers** (any bites are at their own risk), the hunters **don** snake-proof boots and pick their way through the rocky outcrops, shining hand mirrors to glimpse into the nooks and crannies where the usually timid creatures live.

With specially designed tongs and hooks, the hunters probe and prod. If the snakes will not come out of their own accord, the hunters pump petrol fumes from a garden-sprayer through a **6ft** copper tube, smoking the snakes out like badgers in a sett.

A diamond-back will only strike if provoked. It cannot see as such, but senses its prey using the two pits beneath its nostrils, like a thermal-imaging camera. And even then it can only see moving objects. If you chance upon one unexpectedly, the best thing to do is stay still, however hard that may seem. In fact, however, these hunted snakes, roused from their holes, are usually too cold and dopey to react at all, let alone slither away before the crowd of hunters closes in on them.

Back in the arena at Sweetwater, the live captured snakes – thousands of them – are kept in a huge pit, like something from *Indiana Jones and the Temple of Doom*. The punters gawp, breathing in the bitter smell of snake dung and shouting to be heard above the ominous rattling, like a heavy rain on a tin roof.

From here the snakes are taken to be measured and weighed. There are trophies at stake, awarded to those who turned in the largest rattler and the greatest weight of snakes. In the display pit, handlers give demonstrations, provoking the vipers into striking, to the 'oohs' and 'aahs' of the crowd. Their venom is extracted

---

disclaimer: document saying that the organisers are not responsible for any injuries

don: put on

6ft: two metres

in the milking pit, with the handlers holding the snakes' tails between their legs as they press the fangs over a glass funnel.

Then, in a **macabre** piece of theatre, the snakes are beheaded with **machetes**, gutted and skinned. Miss Snake Charmer – the festival's own teenage beauty queen – is ready to assist with the **disembowelling**.

Clutching a butcher's knife, with a tiara on her head and a smile on her lips, she plays to the crowd like a gladiator, wiping her bloody hands on her paper butcher's apron.

The skins are sold wet for $5 a piece.

And the meat? Still twitching, it is put on ice to be deep-fried later. Amid the trailers nearby, a line snakes towards a food stand. Apparently, it tastes just like chicken, only a little more stringy. The biter is well and truly bit.

---

macabre: gruesome
machetes: broad, heavy knives
disembowelling: taking the inside parts out of the snakes

Free fall
Carl dos Santos

Have you imagined the sensation of jumping from an aircraft and simply free-falling through an empty sky, deliberately not opening your parachute until the very last minute? Carl dos Santos describes what it is like.

Standing in the doorway of the plane you still feel grounded. The equipment weighs heavily on your back, the floor presses against your feet, and the straps pull on your legs and shoulders. Longing for the freedom of flight, you leap. Ten seconds after leaving the plane the wind supports you, fighting against gravity, holding you at a constant speed.

Touching nothing but air you feel the exhilarating rush of **adrenaline** as you soar through the sky at 120 miles per hour. You are in control; with the slightest movements of your body you alter heading, speed, and position. You and the invisible element seem perfectly in

adrenaline: a substance that stimulates the nervous system when the body is stressed or excited

tune yet the thrill of danger sharpens your focus, slows time, and heightens your senses. Your every nerve tingles with excitement. That smooth collage of colour miles below may be where you live, but this is where you are most alive! For sixty seconds of eternity you are completely free of all worldly concerns; it is just you and the sky.

With only one mile left to fall, the land has started moving toward you. You now have a glimmer of the immense speed at which you are travelling. As you fall below four thousand feet, the Earth begins to quickly expand, rushing to meet you. Five short seconds later, a scant three thousand feet left, you open that life-saving piece of cloth. The mad rush of wind suddenly transforms into the peaceful calm of a parachute ride. Slowly your ears adjust to the new volume and you hear the flapping of that beautiful fabric above your head. Eventually gravity reasserts itself; you are now below two hundred feet and the Earth is charging up, ready to swallow you. At a mere twelve feet, with a pull on the toggles, you slow your descent and gently set your feet on the ground. You have dared to defy gravity and again you have emerged victorious.

Quest for the Lost World
Brian Blessed

The actor Brian Blessed has always had a craving for adventure, and at one time even tried to climb Mount Everest without oxygen, in the footsteps of his great mountaineering hero, Edward Mallory. A few years ago, he decided to embark on an expedition to find 'The Lost World', the setting for a Jurassic Park*-style novel by Sir Arthur Conan Doyle written in 1912. At the start of their return journey, they set off across the South American forests in a small light aircraft. But they had not gone far before an engine failure meant an emergency landing. The problem was, there was nowhere to land!*

It all sounds insane, I know, but my mind was racing. My frustration grew with every fleeting moment. God in heaven! How bloody boring, I thought, to die in a poky little aeroplane. Ridiculously, I fantasised about dying on some holy quest alongside **Sir Galahad**. This image was then replaced by another as I saw myself reach the summit of Mount Everest with bleeding, broken legs. I imagined sacrificing my life fighting a lion in a Roman arena to save my wife and child.

Then reality bought me back to my senses. The jarring, guttural voice of Captain Ismail Urdaneta rang out across the cabin:

'Strap your seat-belts on! Emergency! Emergency!'

We were about 1000 feet (300 m) above the trees, and because of this the impression of speed was much greater than that experienced higher in the sky. The plane

---

Sir Galahad: one of King Arthur's knights of the Round Table

lurched horribly to the right and dipped precariously downwards.

There was a look of abject terror in the eyes of one of the ladies.

'It's all right,' shouted Nick, 'they'll get us down safely.'

All I could see through my window was jungle. Was Urdaneta going to land us on that or had he, at last, found a clearing? Though his co-pilot was sitting down, he was still standing. From this position he had one hand on the controls and the other on a hand-mike. Into this he shouted, 'Mayday! Mayday! Emergency! Emergency!' and lots of other jargon which I didn't understand. What was alarming was the fact that he was still standing! I could see that he was still searching for a suitable place to land. The poor man was distraught and sweating profusely, yet he still appeared in control of the situation.

It seemed the plane was probably running out of fuel, or that the remaining engine was beginning to malfunction. It was spluttering, but, of course, the Captain may have been shutting it down to redress the balance for a glided landing.

To my delight, large patches of greenery appeared between the trees, but we were still going very fast and the scenery whizzed by at an alarming rate.

Suddenly I had the weird sensation of weightlessness as the plane dropped 50 feet (15 m) or so. We started to dip sharply to the right. Jesus! It was dramatic! And then all hell broke loose! It reminded me of the moment in the film *Apollo 13* when Tom Hanks said from the immense void of space, 'Houston, we have a problem.'

We certainly had a problem. Noises that reminded me of anti-aircraft ack-ack guns, blasted out from the instrument control panel. This unnerving sound finally confirmed to our stunned minds the fact that we really were going to crash.

Orange lights started flashing on and off as if we had won a top prize on a television game show. I was almost tempted to shout, 'Ismail Urdaneta, Come On Down.' Down, down, down we went, and up, up, up came the ground to meet us! I just felt cold and stubborn. No, I thought, I'm damned if I am going to die like this!

I sat myself on the empty seat to my right away from the window and secured the seat-belt, and gripped the back of the seat in front of me. People's voices seemed far away and I felt as if I was moving in a slow motion dream. Across the gangway was a young lady called Janet, who enquired in a matter-of-fact sort of way:

'Brian, what's the brace position?'

I smiled back at her and said, 'Oh sweetheart, just get your head down and hold on to the seat in front of you.'

She did just that, but not before exchanging a loving look with her husband Miles, who was seated behind her.

In front of me on the left the veins on Nick's neck stood out like telegraph wires as he strained his head around to catch a glimpse of his wife, Marianne. She was at the rear of the plane with Anthony, her lips opening and closing in consternation as she returned his gaze. Everyone else seemed to be in the brace position. The remaining married couple, Tim and Karen, were bent over and holding hands. On seeing me sitting upright Anthony shouted, 'Brace yourself, **Challenger**.'

The instruction was taken up by Captain Urdaneta as he finally sat down.

This is it! I thought. This is it! Brace yourselves! I ask you! It all seemed too daft to laugh at.

My mind conjured up the image of Rocky Marciano. (Bear with me! I promise you I haven't lost the plot.) Rocky Marciano? Well, in the early 1950s Marciano was the heavyweight boxing champion of the world. He was 5 feet 10 inches (1.8 m) tall and weighed 13 stone 5.5 pounds (85 kg). Every challenger he fought was bigger than he

---

Challenger: Professor Challenger was the hero of *The Lost World*

was, yet with his awesome power, he terrified and destroyed them all. His famous right hand, which kissed all comers asleep, was affectionately known as the 'Suzy Q'. He was unbeaten for the whole of his career and he was considered indestructible. At the age of 49 he died in a plane crash in the USA. The plane was a small Cessna, not dissimilar in size to the one we were flying. When aviation experts examined the wreckage they found Marciano contorted and mangled in the metal fuselage. His body was discovered in the perfect brace position.

What chance had we got, I thought, if a guy as powerful as Marciano had ended up compressed like a concertina!

With this cheerful thought in my head, we hit the ground. It was a dreadful moment. Bang, thud, wallop! God knows how to describe the sound and to be perfectly honest I can't remember what it sounded like, I simply felt as sick as a dog. **Adrenaline** surged through my body. Yes, we were down, thank God. And miraculously still in one piece. The pilots deserved a lot of brownie points for that.

We were careering along a field of thick high grass like an out-of-control express train. We really were going at a hell of a lick. The scenery outside my window was a blur. The plane shook violently as the two heroic pilots fought desperately to control it. The great danger was that once it stopped the tail end would flip over and cause it to explode. But, thank our lucky stars, this didn't happen.

There was a tremendous thud and the plane came to an abrupt standstill. The impact was so great that I actually tore the seat I was hanging on to out of the floor!

Someone yelled, 'Get out quickly – it can blow up at any minute.'

Adrenaline: a substance that stimulates the nervous system when the body is stressed or excited

The ladies went first, **jettisoning themselves** into the long grass and we, the chaps, followed in quick succession.

'Keep going. Keep going,' urged Nick, 'to hell with the bloody luggage, leave it, it's not important. We have got to get well away from the plane. I've seen one blow up!'

This was all very well and good, but we had landed in a swampy field and were up to our knees in mud and water. This, combined with the long, thick grass, made our progress painfully slow. However, eventually, we reached a safe distance from the plane.

Our commotion through the swamp stirred up clouds of mosquitoes and other 'dive bombers', which set about us with a vengeance. Once more we sampled *el sudar y las moscas*.

These insect swarms were frightful. The mosquitoes seemed to have **proboscises** long and tough enough to pierce bell metal. My bare forearms quickly became a bloody mess, but it was the ladies who suffered the most, Marianne in particular. Thinking that the expedition was over they had not put on their long trousers or protective shirts. Much to Marianne's distress, lumps and bumps appeared all over her arms and legs.

This was all too much, coming so quickly after the crash. We were a group of terrified people in shock. The women wept openly and the men were bent double in an effort to control their emotions. I stood shaking, my video camera in my hand. Andrew Bawn, a delightful Scotsman, exclaimed, 'Bloody hell, Brian, do you mean to say that you have been filming it all?'

'Yes,' I nodded.

He shook his head in absolute disbelief, 'God, you're a cool bugger!'

---

jettisoning themselves: throwing themselves out
el sudar y las moscas: (Spanish) sweat and flies
proboscises: long, flexible mouth-parts of an insect

'Not at all,' I replied, 'I always knew we would get down safely!'

'Yes,' and Andrew, 'And liars are born every minute.'

To which I replied, 'Yes – and this one was born sixty-two years ago.'

We laughed in indescribable relief.

It was then that we realised to our utter amazement that the two pilots had remained beside the aircraft. They stood motionless outside the exit door.

'They're bloody fools,' said Nick, 'they could have been killed.'

After a while, Anthony decided to have a word with them. He set off towards the plane. Meanwhile the sky had filled with tiny white aeroplanes responding to Captain Urdaneta's distress calls. Though there was nothing they could do to assist us, the sight of them cheered us up immensely. We waved enthusiastically to show that we were all right and they continued to circle round. The planes looked so pretty against the dark blue sky. To any Pemon Indians observing them from afar they must have looked like a host of giant white butterflies in search of sweet-scented orchids. The 'orchids' of course were us – and we 'orchids' needed to get a move on. It was 6.30 in the evening and getting dark, and the mosquitoes were increasing in number by the minute.

At this point Anthony beckoned to us shouting, 'It's all right. The Captain says that the plane is safe. It won't blow up. Come and get your luggage and we'll start walking out of here.'

The decision to walk was welcomed by all and was certainly preferable to sitting around in the dark being bitten to death. So ten minutes later we had on our backpacks and were on the move.

Anthony started talking to a friendly Pemon Indian farmer who owned the field that we had landed in and, despite the fact that the plane had damaged a considerable portion of his land, he was sweetness and light. The pilots told us that he would be well compensated and I got the impression that the farmer was actually enjoying every minute of the excitement. It was obviously something he could tell his grandchildren for years to come. Justifiably so – the plane had almost hit him!

Apparently he had been watching it for some time when it suddenly started to head towards him. In blind panic he began to run round his field. Finally, in sheer desperation, he ran for the nearest ditch and took a header into it. It must have looked comical to the mosquitoes!

Anyway, he appeared to be none the worse for his brush with death and guided us for the next half-hour. He took us to a rough track which led to a farm and the beginnings of civilization. Without his help we might have gone in the opposite direction and spent hours in the rain forest. The sense of relief we all felt was plain. It was good to be alive.

Conquering Everest
Rebecca Stephens

Brian Blessed would be envious of Rebecca Stephens. She has done what he failed to do: stood on the summit of the world's highest peak – Mount Everest. In this extract, accompanied by two Himalayan climbers, Kami Tchering and Ang Passang, she embarks on the final stretch of the ascent.

It was about 11.00 a.m. Together we planted my half-used oxygen bottle in the snow, to be collected on our return, and replaced it with a new, full one so that there would be no need to carry a spare, and walked to the summit ridge. I don't know why: I had read hundreds of books and talked to countless people, and yet when I first set eyes on the view along that final ridge towards the summit, it staggered me. Everything we had climbed thus far had been snow and ice, with just a little smidgen of rock peeping through here and there. What lay ahead was rock, mostly: large **angular** lumps, falling away abruptly, left and right. To the left it falls sharply away, 6000 feet into Nepal; and to the right, even more sharply, if that's possible, the 9000 feet of the Kangshung Face, into Tibet.

'You can go first, Kami Tchering,' I said.

'No, you can go.'

'No, you go.'

Kami Tchering led, down a little gully and onto the ridge. It wasn't difficult by Alpine standards; I'd heard it said it was **a mere *peu difficile***, but it was about as

angular: with sharp corners
a mere *peu difficile*: a climb that was only slightly difficult

exposed as you can get. This was Hillary Step territory. I could see it ahead: a large **rhomboid** boulder standing on its head, complicated with slabs and **cornices** all about. But first we had to inch our way along the ridge to that point. On closer inspection, it seemed that for most of the way we could follow a passage on snow. On the right, huge cornices, beaten and swept into shape by the prevailing westerly winds, jutted out like great snowy waves over the 9000-foot drop into Tibet. And from the tips of these waves, the ridge, snow for the most, dropped steeply to join the edge of the rocks atop the western face, falling into Nepal. Along this, we climbed, grabbing a rock hold with our clumsy mittened hands where we could, checking and double checking each step to ensure its stability. Climb too high to the right, stick an ice-axe into the snow for balance, and it would enter in Nepal, to exit the other side of the cornice in Tibet. Climb too low to the left and, well, there was nothing. There were fixed ropes in parts, into which I diligently clipped my harness; but where there were not, one slip and it would all have been over.

Within an hour or so, perhaps less, we were at the foot of Hillary's Step. This, Harry had said, was so **nondescript** that you could climb it without noticing it. In a pair of plimsolls, perhaps; on a warm summer's afternoon, in shorts, bare-fingered, perhaps. But at nearly 29 000 feet, in heavy boots, hands rendered into useless clubs by vast gloves, ice-axe swinging, goggles steaming up, I beg to differ.

A bunch of old tat hung like a knotted loop of multicoloured spaghetti, from some unseen anchor. I grabbed it, pulled, and with a series of inelegant kicks,

---

rhomboid: diamond-shaped
cornices: overhanging masses of hardened snow
nondescript: ordinary and uninteresting

tugs, pushes, rams and elbow shoves, jostled and heaved my clumsy self onto a sloping **mantel**, the top of the rhomboid, I suppose, some two-thirds of the way up the Step. From here it was relatively simple: I planted my axe into a snowy shelf above, and scrambled.

I was glad when we left the rockier part of the ridge behind, for ahead, as before, cornices swept in vast, frozen waves to the right, and steep rocky slopes fell away to the left, into Nepal; the ridge was broader than before, though, more gently inclined, a little kinder. It **undulated** on, as ridges tend to do, one bump, then another, and another.

But there was an air of confidence among us now and despite fatigue, thin air, the effort required to put one foot in front of the other, and the **implausibility** of us

mantel: shelf
undulated: went up and down, like waves
implausibility: unlikely fact

climbing together on the summit ridge of this, Everest, the most majestic mountain of them all, we knew now that we would make it to the summit. And we knew the moment we were about to arrive, for there, ahead, was the highest bump of them all with lots of flags on top. We stood and waited until the three of us were huddled in a little cluster, and together stepped on top of the world. It wasn't very dramatic but the joy on the **Sherpas**' faces made my heart near burst: 'Summit, summit, summit. We make summit!'

Nothing mattered that night. It occurred to me that not once in our five-hour descent had I afforded myself the luxury of thinking that I had just climbed to the top of the world. The concentration of putting one foot slowly in front of the other had been too great. Only now that the storm which had threatened to scupper our chances had finally struck, the wind whistling around the tent, the poles buckling still further and the canvas flapping, did I stop to think that at this final hour we had completed what we had set out to do. I lay, Tcheri Zhambu asleep at my side, and realized that for the first time in my thirty-one years I was quietly, deeply content. Everest had been my first mountain, and surely not my last.

Sherpas: Nepalese or Tibetan people from the Himalayas. They act as guides to mountaineers

Runningman
Robert Garside

Carrying nothing with him but a map, a toothbrush, a change of clothes and £20 in cash, Robert Garside set off from London in 1997 to run round the world. One of the major problems he encountered on his 42 000 mile marathon was being attacked by muggers. But the people he met on the way were not all bad. In this account from his website (www.runningman.org), he recounts a memorable experience in the middle of China. Running through the night, he becomes faint from exhaustion and lack of water...

My eyes became red from the continuous cold air wafting in and the unusual length of time I had been awake and running. Every now and again I stood motionless staring at the ground, closing my eyes to rest them, swaying on my feet, pretending I was sleeping. Then I'd wake myself and my legs up and run on, trying to discipline my thoughts. I was at war for the night, a quiet war of concentration and I had to kid myself that I was escaping from the enemy, which was all part of coping with the long night. It got colder as the night drew on and my body felt quite numb as I plodded mindlessly forwards into yet more uncertainty.

The sun finally started to rise, awakening the town I had been running towards all night. Approaching its outskirts I felt emotionally devastated by what had been one of the toughest points in the run. I hardly noticed I was still moving as my eyelids kept closing, but then shouted out loud as my thirst raged – I did not care about anything else other than water and sleep and I'd do anything to get both.

By 07:00 hrs I had made it to the town centre and early morning workers stared at me. I didn't have the patience of energy for anything, I just headed for the nearest place to get a drink, and that's when a police jeep headed down the main street in my direction. I used the last of my energy sprinting into a back street. If they saw me at this hour I would probably get questioned, so I kept going, turning down some more back streets. My pace slowed drastically to a pathetic jog, I just didn't have anything left, which was probably just as well because the locals might get suspicious. I felt **driven to the wall** and needed sleep so badly that I found it difficult to do anything. I could not concentrate and kept bursting into hysterical laughter. Then I stopped in a corner standing still in a kind of a daze, breathing shallowly through my mouth, holding onto a drain pipe. 'God when will this day end?' I muttered deliriously as I lost my feet, slumping down in the corner by a door. I didn't care, I'd had enough, I just could not do it. My chin dropped to my chest and I don't remember anything else.

Some time later I felt a tapping on my shoulder. It was insistent and became heavier. I raised my chin, my eyes feeling heavier as I squinted upwards at a man frowning. His hand was on my shoulder and he was looking into my eyes as if to see what was wrong with me. He peered closely at me, his old skin gathering up into countless rows of brown wrinkles, as he smiled and nodded, exposing a gold front tooth, which shone in the daylight. It made me laugh – or perhaps it was the stress.

He held out his hand, helping me up onto my stiff legs and I took it, hardly able to walk, my thigh muscles especially objecting. He was faster than I, as he led me inside up some wooden stairs to a room, where there was a made-up bed. I got some translations out of my bag,

---

driven to the wall: at the end of his ability to keep going

showing him. 'Please can I have a cheap bed for the night? I don't have much money,' it read. I did not want to assume anything. He read it and smiled and I took that as a yes.

A woman appeared at the top of the stairs and walked over to me, pointing at me and pulling at her sleeves and rubbing her hands together. Holding out her hands, she was requesting my clothes to wash. I nodded and she walked off, returning with some of her husband's clothes to wear, so I changed and she left to wash mine. Then a young girl requested my shoes, which she washed in front of me in a basin of hot water, taken from flasks. I stared at her, my eyes closing; then I washed my body in sections with a cloth in a separate bowl.

Activities

Snakes and nutters

1 This news report is written using bias: the writer has a strong opinion and this is clear from the way he uses language. For example, the headline `Snakes and nutters` makes it clear that he thinks that the Texans are crazy to do this. Find other expressions that indicate his opinion about the 'Rattlesnake Round-up' and explain the real meaning.

2 In small groups, talk about your opinions of rattlesnake-hunting, as it is described in the article. Use quotations from the article to support your views.

    a Do you think it is:

- a cruel activity that ought to be banned?
- part of the Texan way of life?
- a necessary activity to get rid of a dangerous pest?

    b Is it wrong to:

- dig out sleeping snakes and kill them?
- eat the snake-meat?
- turn the snakeskins into fashion-wear afterwards?

3 Write a letter to the local Sweetwater newspaper, the Argus, either supporting the annual snake-kill, or condemning it as cruel. Use facts from the article, as well as some of the arguments which arose in your discussion.

Free fall

4 Design an advertisement to go in a magazine for young people to encourage them to take up free-falling. Use parts of the description in the article (such as 'Your every nerve tingles with excitement') to make people understand what a thrilling activity it is. You could list the thrills in bullet points.

5 Write your own step-by-step account of an exciting activity. For example, you could write about the thrill of scoring a goal or riding a sled down an icy slope. Follow the same structure as the extract, giving an account of what happens stage-by-stage, or even second-by-second, and describe the thrills you are experiencing.

Quest for the Lost World

6 Brian Blessed uses many different language techniques to describe his experience of a crash-landing in the South American forest. He uses:

- adjectives
- adverbs
- expletives (swear words)
- images
- quotations
- rhetorical questions
- metaphor
- simile
- exclamations
- exaggeration.

Find examples of each of these in the text. Do you think this account would be as effective without all these techniques?

7 What kind of person does Brian Blessed seem to be? In pairs, talk about what you have learned about his personality from the way he tells the story and the comments he makes. For example:

- How does he react to the fact that they are likely to crash?
- What are his feelings about the prospect of dying?
- What is his attitude towards the women on the expedition?
- What would you say about his sense of humour?

8 Write your own account of an emergency, showing how different people react. You could base your story on a real expedition, such as Scott's journey to the South Pole, or invent a situation of your own, setting it in a hospital, perhaps, or on the sportsfield. Make sure that your narrator's personality shows through, as Brian Blessed's does here.

Conquering Everest

9 Any account of an activity such as mountaineering is bound to include some specialist terms.

    a Write down each of the terms with the correct definition from the list on the right.

mantel	with sharp corners
Sherpas	a climb that was only slightly difficult
a *peu difficile*	diamond-shaped
angular	overhanging masses of hardened snow
cornices	shelf
rhomboid	Nepalese or Tibetan people from the Himalayas

    b Make a list of the main specialist terms from any activity you have been involved in. You could choose a sport, such as cricket or horse-riding, a hobby or a science, such as the equipment needed for physics. Then write clear definitions which a non-expert could understand.

10 Write a simplified version of Rebecca Stephens's account for readers aged between six and seven. Use short sentences and keep the vocabulary as simple as possible. At the end, add a glossary which explains the specialist terms that you have used. This might include words such as *oxygen*, *summit*, *Nepal*, *Tibet* and *descent*.

Runningman

11 Robert Garside manages to convey his exhaustion and his poor physical condition in a number of ways. For example, he uses these abstract nouns to identify the qualities that a long-distance runner needs, and which he is lacking: concentration, patience, energy, pace. He also makes effective use of adjectives and adverbs in the first three paragraphs to explain how bad he is feeling. Find the adjectives used to describe these nouns: eyes, air, body, jog; and the adverbs used to tell us more about these verbs: stood, plodded, slowed, muttered.

12 Write the account of his stay in the Chinese family's home from the young woman's point of view. What does she say about this strange foreign traveller? Write her account of how the family helped the runner and then add a section in which she asks herself some questions about him.

Comparing the extracts

13 Write a newspaper report of the events described in any one of these extracts. Give it an eye-catching headline, include a section explaining the background, and give a brief account of the incident. Include quotes from people involved: some can be taken direct from the passage; others might have to be made up.

14 What is the point of 'living dangerously', like the people involved in the activities described in this section? Why do people take part in snake-hunting, free-fall parachuting or expeditions to find the Lost World? Why do they climb Everest or run round the globe?

Hold a class debate in which one side argues that dangerous activities of this kind are pointless, while the other side explains why people get involved in them. First, look back through the extracts to find as many points as you can to support your side of the argument. Then add ideas about other dangerous activities that you have read about or seen on television, such as pot-holing or white-water canoeing.

15 Write an article for a magazine with the title 'Living Dangerously'. Explain why people get involved in activities like the ones described in this section. If you have had a class discussion, you could use some of the arguments that people put forward.

Fighting for freedom

Nobody today would consider themselves truly free unless they had the right to vote when they are old enough, to govern themselves, to work, and to be treated equally, regardless of their sex or the colour of their skins. This section is about individuals and groups of people who have fought – each in their own way – for a basic right that was denied them.

Votes for women
Emmeline Pankhurst

When the Great War started in 1914, women in Britain were still fighting for the right to vote. Their struggle had been led since 1903 by Emmeline Pankhurst, whose Women's Social and Political Union came to be known as the 'suffragettes'. They interrupted political meetings, smashed shop windows in the centre of London and did everything they could to draw attention to their cause. In this extract Emmeline Pankhurst describes the first of the many suffragettes' demonstrations.

At length the opening day of Parliament arrived. On February 19, 1906, occurred the first **suffrage** procession in London. I think there were between three and four hundred women in that procession, poor working-women from the East End, for the most part, leading the

---

suffrage: the right to vote

way in which numberless women of every rank were
afterward to follow. My eyes were misty with tears as I saw
them, standing in line, holding the simple banners which
my daughter Sylvia had decorated, waiting for the word of
command. Of course our procession attracted a large
crowd of intensely amused spectators. The police,
however, made no attempt to disperse our ranks, but
merely ordered us to **furl** our banners. There was no
reason why we should not have carried banners but the
fact that we were women, and therefore could be bullied.
So, bannerless, the procession entered Caxton Hall. To
my amazement it was filled with women, most of whom
I had never seen at any suffrage gathering before.

Our meeting was most enthusiastic, and while Annie
Kenney was speaking, to frequent applause, the news
came to me that the King's speech (which is not the
King's at all, but the formally announced Government
programme for the session) had been read, and that
there was in it no mention of the women's suffrage
question. As Annie took her seat I arose and made this
announcement, and I moved a resolution that the
meeting should at once proceed to the House of
Commons to urge the members to introduce a suffrage
measure. The resolution was carried, and we rushed out
in a body and hurried toward **the Strangers' Entrance**.

It was pouring rain and bitterly cold, yet no one turned
back, even when we learned at the entrance that for the first
time in memory the doors of the House of Commons were
barred to women. We sent in our cards to members who
were personal friends, and some of them came out and
urged our admittance. The police, however, **were obdurate**.

---

furl: fold up
the Strangers' Entrance: the door through which the public are
allowed to enter
were obdurate: refused to change their minds

They had their orders. The Liberal government, **advocates of** the people's rights, had given orders that women should no longer set foot in their stronghold.

Pressure from members proved too great, and the government **relented** to the extent of allowing twenty women at a time to enter the lobby. Through all the rain and cold these hundreds of women waited for hours their turn to enter. Some never got in, and for those of us who did there was small satisfaction. Not a member could be persuaded to take up our cause.

Out of the disappointment and dejection of that experience I yet reaped a richer harvest of happiness than I had ever known before. Those women had followed me to the House of Commons. They had defied the police. They were awake at last. They were prepared to do something that women had never done before – fight for themselves. Women had always fought for men, and for their children. Now they were ready to fight for their own human rights. Our **militant** movement was established.

In 1918 all women over the age of thirty were given the vote. All women were given the same voting rights as men in 1928, a month after Emmeline Pankhurst's death.

---

advocates of: supporters of
relented: gave in
militant: willing to fight

Freedom for India
Webb Miller

In the middle of the twentieth century, many countries which had been part of the old British Empire wanted independence from British rule. India's struggle for freedom was led by Mahatma Gandhi, who organised a series of campaigns which involved civil disobedience – the deliberate breaking of unjust laws. Gandhi believed firmly that victory could be achieved by non-violent means. But this kind of resistance demanded great courage and determination, as the following report, by an American journalist, shows. It is May 1930; Gandhi is in prison, and a group of his followers has embarked upon a protest march against a salt tax.

After plodding about six miles across country lugging a pack of sandwiches and two quart bottles of water under a sun which was already blazing hot, inquiring from every native I met, I reached the assembling place of the Gandhi followers. Several long, open, thatched sheds were surrounded by high cactus thickets. The sheds were literally swarming and buzzed like a beehive with some 2500 Congress or Gandhi men dressed in the regulation uniform of rough homespun cotton *dhotis* and triangular Gandhi caps, somewhat like American overseas soldiers' hats. They chattered excitedly and when I arrived hundreds surrounded me, with evidences of hostility at first. After they learned my identity, I was warmly welcomed by young college-educated, English-speaking men and escorted to **Mme** Naidu. The famous Indian

---

dhotis: loin-cloths, worn around the hips
Mme: short for Madam

poetess, stocky, swarthy, strong-featured, bare-legged, dressed in rough, dark homespun robe and sandals, welcomed me. She explained that she was busy **marshalling** her forces for the demonstration against the salt pans and would talk with me more at length later. She was educated in England and spoke English fluently.

Mme Naidu called for prayer before the march started and the entire assemblage knelt. She exhorted them, 'Gandhi's body is in gaol but his soul is with you. India's **prestige** is in your hands. You must not use any violence under any circumstances. You will be beaten but you must not resist; you must not even raise a hand to ward off blows.' Wild, shrill cheers terminated her speech.

Slowly and in silence the throng commenced the half-mile march to the salt deposits. A few carried ropes for lassoing the barbed-wire stockade around the salt pans. About a score who were assigned to act as stretcher-bearers wore crude, hand-painted red crosses pinned to their breasts; their stretchers consisted of blankets. Manilal Gandhi, second son of Gandhi, walked among the foremost of the marchers. As the throng drew near the salt pans they commenced chanting the revolutionary slogan, *Inquilab zindabad*, intoning the two words over and over.

The salt deposits were surrounded by ditches filled with water and guarded by 400 native Surat police in khaki shorts and brown turbans. Half-a-dozen British officials commanded them. The police carried *lathis* – five-foot clubs tipped with steel. Inside the stockade twenty-five native riflemen were drawn up.

In complete silence the Gandhi men drew up and halted a hundred yards from the stockade. A picked column advanced from the crowd, waded the ditches,

---

marshalling: moving people into position
prestige: reputation

and approached the barbed-wire stockade, which the Surat police surrounded, holding their clubs at the ready. Police officials ordered the marchers to disperse under a recently imposed regulation which prohibited gatherings of more than five persons in any one place. The column silently ignored the warning and slowly walked forward. I stayed with the main body about a hundred yards from the stockade.

Suddenly, at a word of command, scores of native police rushed upon the advancing marchers and rained blows on their heads with their steel-shod *lathis*. Not one of the marchers even raised an arm to fend off the blows. They went down like ten-pins. From where I stood I heard the sickening whacks of the clubs on unprotected skulls. The waiting crowd of watchers groaned and sucked in their breaths in sympathetic pain at every blow.

Those struck down fell sprawling, unconscious or writhing in pain with fractured skulls or broken shoulders. In two or three minutes the ground was quilted with bodies. Great patches of blood widened on their white clothes. The survivors without breaking ranks silently and doggedly marched on until struck down. When every one of the first column had been knocked down stretcher-bearers rushed up **unmolested** by the police and carried off the injured to a thatched hut which had been arranged as a temporary hospital.

Then another column formed while the leaders pleaded with them to retain their self-control. They marched slowly toward the police. Although every one knew that within a few minutes he would be beaten down, perhaps killed, I could detect no signs of wavering or fear. They marched steadily with heads up, without the encouragement of music or cheering or any possibility that they might escape serious injury or death. The police

---

unmolested: undisturbed; not interfered with

rushed out and methodically and mechanically beat down the second column. There was no fight, no struggle; the marchers simply walked forward until struck down. There were no outcries, only groans after they fell. There were not enough stretcher-bearers to carry off the wounded; I saw eighteen injured being carried off simultaneously, while forty-two still lay bleeding on the ground awaiting stretcher-bearers. The blankets used as stretchers were sodden with blood . . .

In the middle of the morning VJ Patel arrived. He had been leading the Swaraj movement since Gandhi's arrest, and had just resigned as President of the Indian Legislative Assembly in protest against the British. Scores surrounded him, knelt, and kissed his feet. He was a **venerable** gentleman of about sixty with white flowing beard and moustache, dressed in the usual undyed, coarse homespun smock. Sitting on the ground under a mango tree, Patel said, 'All hope of reconciling India with the British Empire is lost for ever. I can understand any government's taking people into custody and punishing them for breaches of the law, but I cannot understand how any government that calls itself civilised could deal as savagely and brutally with non-violent, unresisting men as the British have this morning.'

By eleven the heat reached 116 degrees in the shade and the activities of the Gandhi volunteers subsided. I went back to the temporary hospital to examine the wounded. They lay in rows on the bare ground in the shade of an open, palm-thatched shed. I counted 320 injured, many still insensible with fractured skulls, others writhing in agony from kicks in the testicles and stomach. The Gandhi men had been able to gather only a few native doctors, who were doing the best they could with the inadequate facilities. Scores of the injured had

---

venerable: old and respected

received no treatment for hours and two had died. The demonstration was finished for the day on account of the heat.

I was the only foreign correspondent who had witnessed the amazing scene – a classic example of *satyagraha* or non-violent civil disobedience.

India gained independence in 1947. A year later, the 78-year-old Gandhi was assassinated by a Hindu extremist.

The right to work
Wal Hannington

By the early 1930s there was widespread unemployment in Britain, especially in the north of England. In this desperate situation, a group was formed called the National Unemployed Workers' Movement. Their aim was to walk to London, from all parts of the country, and meet in Hyde Park. After that they would march to the House of Commons and present a petition. Their long journeys on foot towards the capital have come to be known as the Hunger Marches. Wal Hannington takes up the story on the final day of the marches in October 1932.

Next morning, 27th October, the general public of London, emerging into the streets, found that special constables had taken over all the normal duties of the policemen on patrol and on traffic duty. This was a clear indication of the elaborate preparations for struggle which the police had made. By mid-day approximately 100 000 London workers were moving towards Hyde Park from all parts of London, to give the greatest welcome to the hunger marchers that had ever been seen in Hyde Park. By two o'clock Hyde Park and the streets around Marble Arch were black with the multitude of workers who had arrived and were now awaiting the arrival of the hunger marchers. It is estimated that 5000 police and **special constables** were gathered round the park, with many thousands more mobilised in the neighbourhood in readiness for action.

The press had announced that morning that all leave

---

special constables: part-time, volunteer policemen

had been stopped for the Coldstream Guards in Wellington barracks, and that they were being held in readiness in case of trouble. As the various **contingents** of marchers began to enter the park at 2.30 there were signs of tremendous enthusiasm. London's warmest welcome, shouted from 100 000 throats in Hyde Park, was the working-class reply to the impudent campaign of lies by the **capitalist press** against the marchers.

As the last contingent of marchers entered the park gates, trouble broke out with the police. It started with the special constables; not being used to their task, they lost their heads, and, as the crowds swept forward on to the space where the meetings were to be held, the specials drew their truncheons in an effort to control the sea of surging humanity. This incensed the workers; they felt particularly bitter towards the specials, whom they had dubbed 'blackleg cops'. The workers turned on the

---

contingents: groups
capitalist press: the newspapers owned by wealthy men
blackleg: someone who carries on working while others are on strike

special constables and put them to flight, but the fighting which they had been responsible for starting continued throughout the whole afternoon, whilst speakers from the marchers were addressing huge gatherings on the green.

The workers kept the police back from the meetings; several times mounted police charged forward, only to be repulsed by thousands of workers who tore up railings and used them as weapons and barricades for the protection of their meetings. Many mounted men were dragged from their horses. From the streets the fighting extended into the park and back again into the streets, where repeated mounted police charges at full speed failed to dislodge the workers. The foot police were on several occasions surrounded by strong forces of workers, and terrific fights ensued. Many workers and police were injured. Inside the park one could hear the roar of the crowd as they fought **tenaciously** around the Marble Arch and along Oxford Street. At one **juncture** a plain-clothes detective stepped forward to speak to a chief inspector; as he did so a **zealous** special constable struck him down with a terrific blow on the head with a staff. He was about to kick him as he lay on the ground, but was prevented from doing so by the officer in uniform, who stepped forward to reprimand him for the

---

tenaciously: without giving way; standing firm
juncture: point in time
zealous: enthusiastic

The struggle for equality

The fight for racial equality has been long and hard, and it is not over yet. Many men and women have dedicated their lives to this struggle, but one of the best known is Martin Luther King. He was born in 1929 in Georgia, one of the southern states of America, and was to become the leader of the black civil rights movement in the 1950s and 60s. The first entry is from The Oxford Children's Encyclopedia.

KING, Martin Luther

Born 1929 in Atlanta, Georgia, USA. He led the black civil rights movement in the USA in the 1950s and 1960s.
Assassinated 1968 aged 39

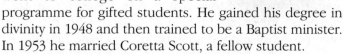

At the age of 15 Martin Luther King went to college on a special programme for gifted students. He gained his degree in divinity in 1948 and then trained to be a Baptist minister. In 1953 he married Coretta Scott, a fellow student.

He became a pastor in Montgomery, Alabama, two years later. Straight away he joined the struggle for black people's rights. The buses in Montgomery had separate seats for blacks and whites, and black people were supposed to stand to let white people sit. Led by King, the blacks boycotted the buses. They shared cars or walked to work until the bus company gave in and allowed all passengers to sit anywhere.

This victory convinced King that the best way for black people to win their rights was to break laws in a non-violent way. In Atlanta and Birmingham, he led 'sit-ins' by blacks in 'whites only' eating places. In spite of being attacked, arrested and imprisoned, King and his followers kept up their campaign. They gained so much support that in August 1963, 200 000 people joined their march on Washington. It was at the rally after this march that he gave his famous 'I have a dream' speech which inspired millions of people throughout the world to campaign for civil rights. Here is an extract:

'I have a dream that one day this nation will rise up and live out the true meaning of its creed: "We hold these truths to be self-evident; that all men are created equal." I have a dream that one day on the red hills of Georgia the sons of former slaves and the sons of former slave-owners will be able to sit down together at the table of brotherhood. I have a dream that my four little children will one day live in a nation where they will not be judged by the color of their skin but by the content of their character.'

The next year the Civil Rights Bill was made law and King was given the Nobel Peace Prize for his work. However, he then began to be opposed by other black leaders who believed that blacks should fight violence with violence. He also became unpopular with some people, especially the government, because he opposed the war in Vietnam.

Then in 1968 he visited Memphis, Tennessee and was killed by a sniper. Only the night before his death, King told his audience: 'I may not get to the promised land with you, but I want you to know tonight that we as a people will.'

The Montgomery bus boycott is described more fully in this extract from the Encarta Encyclopedia *on CD-ROM.*

The Montgomery bus boycott

Montgomery's black community had long-standing grievances about the mistreatment of blacks on city buses. Many white bus drivers treated blacks rudely, often cursing them and humiliating them by enforcing the city's segregation laws, which forced black riders to sit in the back of buses and give up their seats to white passengers on crowded buses. By the early 1950s Montgomery's blacks had discussed boycotting the buses in an effort to gain better treatment – but not necessarily to end **segregation**.

On December 1, 1955, Rosa Parks, a leading member of the local branch of the National Association for the Advancement of Colored People (NAACP), was ordered by a bus driver to give up her seat to a white passenger. When she refused she was arrested and taken to jail. Local leaders of the NAACP, especially Edgar D Nixon, recognized that the arrest of the popular and highly respected Parks was the event that could rally local blacks to a bus protest.

Nixon also believed that a citywide protest should be led by someone who could unify the community. Unlike Nixon and other leaders in Montgomery's black community, the recently arrived King had no enemies. Furthermore, Nixon saw King's public-speaking gifts as great assets in the battle for black civil rights in Montgomery. King was soon chosen as president of the Montgomery Improvement Association (MIA), the organization that directed the bus boycott.

---

segregation: a system of official policies to separate black people from white people and to treat them unfairly

The Montgomery bus boycott lasted for more than a year, demonstrating a new spirit of protest among Southern blacks. King's serious demeanor and consistent appeal to Christian brotherhood and American idealism made a positive impression on whites outside the South. Incidents of violence against black protesters, including the bombing of King's home, focused media attention on Montgomery. In February 1956 an attorney for the MIA filed a lawsuit in **federal** court seeking an **injunction** against Montgomery's segregated seating practices. The federal court ruled in favor of the MIA, ordering the city's buses to be desegregated, but the city government appealed the ruling to the United States Supreme Court. By the time the Supreme Court upheld the lower court decision in November 1956, King was a national figure. His memoir of the bus boycott, *Stride Toward Freedom* (1958), provided a thoughtful account of that experience and further extended King's national influence.

---

federal: in the United States, national as opposed to state
injunction: legal order

Activities

Votes for women

1 In this piece, Emmeline Pankhurst uses a number of expressions deliberately designed to make the reader sympathise with the suffragettes and feel angry at the authorities. Pick out one of these expressions and explain how it achieves its effect.

2 Reread Emmeline Pankhurst's account and note down the major successes for the suffragettes on that day. Then draw up a leaflet advertising another rally. Encourage new recruits by including details of what happened on the February 1906 demonstration, and telling them what can be achieved through more action of this kind in the future.

3 Write a newspaper report of the activities of 19 February 1906 from the point of view of either a male journalist employed by a male newspaper-owner or a woman writing for a pro-suffragette magazine. Include a selection of the details from Emmeline Pankhurst's account.

Freedom for India

4 Webb Miller tells us that the salt deposits were guarded by '400 native Surat police in khaki shorts and brown turbans'. Write out the official report that the police captain had to make after the incident. How would he describe the procession? Would he relate exactly what happened? What would he write about the police response to the procession?

5 Imagine that you were a reporter for an Indian newspaper at that time. Write a feature article about the poet, Madam Naidu, in which you give her brief account of the incident at the salt deposits and she explains Gandhi's philosophy of non-violent civil disobedience.

The right to work

6 This report shows elements of bias in favour of London's workers and against the arrangements that the police made for dealing with the Hunger Marchers. Find phrases that show support for the marchers' cause and others that are critical of the police action.

7 Write a letter from one of the marchers to someone at home. Explain why you went on the march and what happened in London. Share your feelings about the behaviour of the police and the 'blackleg cops'.

8 Draft the script of a radio news item on the marchers' arrival in London. Report on brief interviews with some of the marchers and also with the police, including one of the officers involved in the incident recounted at the end of the extract.

The struggle for equality

9 This encyclopedia entry is divided into two sections: the first provides key facts about Martin Luther King and the second is a much more detailed chronological account of his life. Take the topic sentence (the first one) from each paragraph and use them to write a more detailed key fact section about King's life.

10 Make notes of the main facts from the two articles, with dates. Then represent them in a 'Martin Luther King time-line' from 1948 to 1968. Draw up a final version of the time-line to use as an attractive wall chart.

11 Redraft the account of the Montgomery bus boycott as an additional entry in the children's encyclopedia. Keep the language simple and include only the main facts.

Comparing the extracts

12 Emmeline Pankhurst and the suffragettes waged a campaign which involved smashing shop windows; Gandhi's demonstrators were breaking laws which limited the number of people who could attend demonstrations; the Hunger Marchers fought the police; and Martin Luther King's followers broke many segregation laws in their pursuit of civil rights.

Hold a class discussion about when it is right – if it ever is – to break the law. Refer to these examples and others that you might know about, such as animal-rights activists. Ask yourselves questions such as:

- If law-breaking is always wrong, what should the 'freedom-fighters' in this section have done instead, to achieve their aims?
- If law-breaking can sometimes be right, or acceptable, what 'rules' would you lay down to help people judge when it is acceptable to break the law?

13 Look back at the encyclopedia entry on Martin Luther King. Then write an entry for a children's encyclopedia on one of the following:

- Emmeline Pankhurst and the suffragettes
- the Hunger Marchers
- Gandhi and civil disobedience.

You will find many of the basic facts that you need in this section, but you will need to do some further research. You can get more information from encyclopedias, CD-ROMs and the Internet.

Two viewpoints

No two people view the world in the same way. One person is able to laugh at life's problems; another becomes angry and bitter. Bill Bryson and George Orwell both write about the people around them and the society in which they live. But, while Bryson takes a light-hearted view of his experiences, Orwell's view is serious and critical.

George Orwell

George Orwell, who died in 1950, is best known for his novels *Animal Farm*, in which pigs lead a revolution against their human masters, and *1984*, a grim picture of a society in which no one is free to have their own thoughts. But he also wrote a great many short essays, extracts from three of which are printed here.

A hanging

As a young man in the 1920s Orwell served with the Indian Imperial Police in Burma, and he later used his experiences as the basis for his first novel, Burmese Days. *In this essay, which he wrote under his real name of Eric Blair, he describes having to be present at an execution. It is typical of Orwell to be struck by the small details in a moment of tension and high drama.*

One prisoner had been brought out of his cell. He was a Hindu, a puny wisp of a man, with a shaven head and vague liquid eyes. He had a thick, sprouting moustache, absurdly too big for his body, rather like the moustache of a comic man on the films. Six tall Indian warders were guarding him and getting him ready for the gallows. Two of them stood by with rifles and fixed bayonets, while the others handcuffed him, passed a chain through his handcuffs and fixed it to their belts, and lashed his arms tight to his sides. They crowded very close about him, with their hands always on him in a careful, caressing grip, as though all the while feeling him to make sure he was there. It was like men handling a fish which is still alive and may jump back into the water. But he stood quite unresisting, yielding his arms limply to the ropes, as though he hardly noticed what was happening.

Eight o'clock struck and a bugle call, desolately thin in the wet air, floated from the distant barracks. The superintendent of the jail, who was standing apart from the rest of us, moodily prodding the gravel with his stick, raised his head at the sound. He was an army doctor, with a grey toothbrush moustache and a gruff voice. 'For God's sake hurry up, Francis,' he said irritably. 'The man ought to have been dead by this time. Aren't you ready yet?'

Francis, the head jailer, a fat **Dravidian** in a white drill suit and gold spectacles, waved his black hand. 'Yes sir, yes sir,' he bubbled. 'All iss satisfactorily prepared. The hangman iss waiting. We shall proceed.'

'Well, quick march, then. The prisoners can't get their breakfast till this job's over.'

We set out for the gallows. Two warders marched on either side of the prisoner, with their rifles at the slope; two others marched close against him, gripping him by arm and shoulder, as though at once pushing and supporting him. The rest of us, magistrates and the like, followed behind. Suddenly, when we had gone ten yards, the procession stopped short without any order or warning. A dreadful thing had happened – a dog, come goodness knows whence, had appeared in the yard. It came bounding among us with a loud volley of barks, and leapt round us wagging its whole body, wild with glee at finding so many human beings together. It was a large woolly dog, half Airedale, half **pariah**. For a moment it pranced round us, and then, before anyone could stop it, it had made a dash for the prisoner, and jumping up tried to lick his face. Everyone stood aghast, too taken aback even to grab at the dog.

'Who let that bloody brute in here?' said the superintendent angrily. 'Catch it, someone!'

A warder, detached from the escort, charged clumsily after the dog, but it danced and gambolled just out of his reach, taking everything as part of the game. A young Eurasian jailer picked up a handful of gravel and tried to stone the dog away, but it dodged the stones and came after us again. Its yaps echoed from the jail walls. The prisoner, in the grasp of the two warders, looked on incuriously, as though this was another formality of the hanging. It was several minutes before someone

---

Dravidian: a man from the south of India or Sri Lanka
pariah: a half-wild dog

managed to catch the dog. Then we put my handkerchief through its collar and moved off once more, with the dog still straining and whimpering.

It was about forty yards to the gallows. I watched the bare brown back of the prisoner marching in front of me. He walked clumsily with his bound arms, but quite steadily, with that bobbing gait of the Indian who never straightens his knees. At each step his muscles slid neatly into place, the lock of hair on his scalp danced up and down, his feet printed themselves on the wet gravel. And once, in spite of the men who gripped him by each shoulder, he stepped slightly aside to avoid a puddle on the path.

It is curious, but till that moment I had never realized what it means to destroy a healthy, conscious man. When I saw the prisoner step aside to avoid the puddle, I saw the mystery, the unspeakable wrongness, of cutting a life short when it is in full tide. This man was not dying, he was alive just as we were alive. All the organs of his body were working – bowels digesting food, skin renewing itself, nails growing, tissues forming – all toiling away in solemn foolery. His nails would still be growing when he stood on the drop, when he was falling through the air with a tenth of a second to live. His eyes saw the yellow gravel and the grey walls, and his brain still remembered, foresaw, reasoned – reasoned even about puddles. He and we were a party of men walking together, seeing, hearing, feeling, understanding the same world; and in two minutes, with a sudden snap, one of us would be gone – one mind less, one world less.

A sniper in the trenches

In the 1930s a civil war broke out in Spain. Orwell was among many British men and women who went off to join the Republican side, in an attempt to defeat the

Fascists (a party which shared many policies with Hitler's Nazis). Here he describes a brief moment from that war. Armed with a rifle, he has been stationed in a trench as a sniper. His job is to keep a look out and shoot at any enemy soldier who appears out of the opposing trenches. What happens then reminds him that the 'enemy' is made up of ordinary human beings like himself.

Early one morning another man and I had gone out to snipe at the Fascists in the trenches outside Huesca. Their line and ours here lay three hundred yards apart, at which range our aged rifles would not shoot accurately, but by sneaking out to a spot about a hundred yards from the Fascist trench you might, if you were lucky, get a shot at someone through a gap in the **parapet**. Unfortunately the ground between was a flat beet-field with no cover except a few ditches, and it was necessary to go out while it was still dark and return soon after dawn, before the light became too good. This time no Fascists appeared, and we stayed too long and were caught by the dawn. We were in a ditch, but behind us were two hundred yards of flat ground with hardly enough cover for a rabbit. We were still trying to nerve ourselves to make a dash for it when there was an uproar and a blowing of whistles in the Fascist trench. Some of our aeroplanes were coming over. At this moment a man, presumably carrying a message to an officer, jumped out of the trench and ran along the top of the parapet in full view. He was half-dressed and was holding up his trousers with both hands as he ran. **I refrained from** shooting at him. It is true that I am a poor shot and unlikely to hit a running man at a hundred yards, and also that I was thinking chiefly about getting back to our trench while the Fascists had their

---

parapet: low earth wall along the top of a trench
I refrained from: I stopped myself

attention fixed on the aeroplanes. Still, I did not shoot partly because of that detail about the trousers. I had come here to shoot at 'Fascists'; but a man who is holding up his trousers isn't a 'Fascist', he is visibly a fellow creature, similar to yourself, and you don't feel like shooting at him.

What does this incident demonstrate? Nothing very much, because it is the kind of thing that happens all the time in all wars.

The sporting spirit

Orwell did not live to see the behaviour of hooligans at major football championships in recent years. Had he done so, it would have confirmed all his doubts about international sport. In 1945 the Moscow Dynamo football team toured England, playing against a number of the best teams around at that time. The event proved to Orwell that international matches of this kind could only serve to worsen relations between the countries involved. This is the conclusion to his essay, 'The sporting spirit'.

If you wanted to add to the vast fund of ill-will existing in the world at the moment, you could hardly do it better than by a series of football matches between Jews and Arabs, Germans and Czechs, Indians and British, Russians and Poles, and Italians and Jugoslavs, each match to be watched by a mixed audience of 100 000 spectators. I do not, of course, suggest that sport is one of the main causes of international rivalry; big-scale sport is itself, I think, merely another effect of the causes that have produced nationalism. Still, you do make things worse by sending forth a team of eleven men, labelled as national champions, to do battle against some rival team, and allowing it to be felt on all sides that whichever nation is defeated will 'lose face'.

I hope, therefore, that we shan't follow up the visit of the Dynamos by sending a British team to the **USSR**. If we must do so, then let us send a second-rate team which is sure to be beaten and cannot be claimed to represent Britain as a whole. There are quite enough real causes of trouble already, and we need not add to them by encouraging young men to kick each other on the shins amid the roars of infuriated spectators.

USSR: The Union of Soviet Socialist Republics (since broken up into many countries, the largest being the Russian Federation)

Bill Bryson

You have already met Bill Bryson's writing in Section 2. He is an American travel writer who lived for nearly twenty years in Britain before returning to the United States in the early 1990s. As someone who has lived in two societies, he is able to see the oddities in each, and he has described them in several books. These include *Notes from a Small Island* (his account of a journey around Britain) and *Notes from a Big Country* (reports of what he found on his return to the United States).

At the barber's

Many people have had bad experiences at the hairdresser's. As Bill Bryson says, 'If there is one thing

I have learned, it is that a barber will give you the haircut he wants to give you and there is nothing you can do about it.' In this extract, he has gone in for 'just a simple tidy-up', but, as he dreads, the barber has other ideas.

He nods thoughtfully, in a way that makes me realize we are not even in the same universe taste-in-hairwise, and says in a sudden, decisive tone: 'I know just what you want. We call it the Wayne Newton.'

'That's really not quite what I had in mind,' I start to protest, but already he is pushing my chin into my chest and seizing up his shears.

'It's a very popular look – everyone on the bowling team has it,' he adds, and with a buzz of motors starts taking hair off my head as if stripping wallpaper.

'I really don't want the Wayne Newton look,' I murmur with feeling, but my chin is buried in my chest and in any case my voice is drowned in the hum of his dancing clippers.

And so I sit for a small, tortured eternity, staring at my lap, under strict instructions not to move, listening to terrifying cutting machinery trundling across my scalp. Out of the corner of my eyes I can see large quantities of shorn hair tumbling onto my shoulders.

'Not too much off,' I bleat from time to time, but he is engaged in a lively conversation with the barber and customer at the next chair about the prospects for the Chicago Bulls basketball team, and only occasionally turns his attention to me and my head, generally to mutter, 'Oh, dang,' or 'Whoopsie'.

Eventually he jerks my head up and says: 'How's that for length?'

I squint at the mirror, but without my glasses all I can see is what looks like a pink balloon in the distance.

'I don't know,' I say. 'It looks awfully short.'

I notice he is looking unhappily at everything above my eyebrows. 'Did we decide on a Paul Anka or a Wayne Newton?' he asks.

'Well, neither, as a matter of fact,' I say, pleased to have an opportunity to get this sorted out at last. 'I just wanted a modest tidy-up.'

'Let me ask you this,' he says. 'How fast does your hair grow?'

'Not very,' I say and squint harder at the mirror, but I still can't see a thing. 'Why, is there a problem?'

'Oh, no,' he says, but in that way that means 'Oh, yes'. 'No, it's fine,' he goes on. 'It's just that I seem to have done the left side of your head in a Paul Anka and the right in a Wayne Newton. Let me ask you this, then: do you have a big hat?'

'What have you done?' I ask in a rising tone of alarm, but he has gone off to his colleagues for a consultation. They look at me the way you might look at a road accident victim, and talk in whispers.

'I think it must be these **antihistamines** I'm taking,' I hear Thumbs say to them sadly.

One of the colleagues comes up for a closer look, and decides it's not as disastrous as it looks. 'If you take some of this hair here from behind the left ear,' he says, 'and take it around the back of his head and hook it over the other ear, and maybe reattach some of this from here, then you can make it into a modified Barney Rubble.' He turns to me. 'Will you be going out much over the next few weeks, sir?'

'Did you say "Barney Rubble"?' I whimper in dismay.

'Unless you go for a Hercules Poirot,' suggests the other barber.

'Hercules Poirot?' I whimper anew.

They leave Thumbs to do what he can. After another ten minutes he hands me my glasses and lets me raise my

---

antihistamines: tablets that make you drowsy, taken for allergies

head. In the mirror I am confronted with an image that brings to mind a lemon meringue pie with ears. Over my shoulder, Thumbs is smiling proudly.

'Turned out pretty good after all, eh?' he says.

I am unable to speak. I hand him a large sum of money and stumble from the shop. I walk home with my collar up and my head sunk into my shoulders.

Farmers

Barbers, it seems, are not the only professionals who have problems with sharp implements. Here Bill Bryson reflects on why it is that so many farmers seem to have fingers missing.

It is a little-noticed fact that most farmers have parts missing off them. This used to trouble me when I was small. For a long time I assumed that it was because of the hazards of farming life. After all, farmers deal with lots of dangerous machinery. But when you think about it, a lot of people deal with dangerous machinery, and only a tiny proportion of them ever suffer permanent injury. Yet there is scarcely a farmer in the Midwest over the age of twenty who has not at some time or other had a limb or digit yanked off and thrown into the next field by some noisy farmyard implement. To tell you the absolute truth, I think farmers do it on purpose. I think working day after day beside these massive threshers and balers with their grinding gears and flapping fan belts and complex mechanisms they get a little hypnotised by all the noise and motion. They stand there staring at the whirring machinery and they think, 'I wonder what would happen if I just stuck my finger in there a little bit.' I know that sounds crazy. But you have to realise that farmers don't have a whole lot of sense in these matters because they feel no pain.

It's true. Every day in the *Des Moines Register* you can find a story about a farmer who has inadvertently torn off an arm and then calmly walked six miles into the nearest town to have it sewn back on. The stories always say, 'Jones, clutching his severed limb, told his physician, "I seem to have cut my durn arm off, Doc"'. It's never 'Jones, spurting blood, jumped around hysterically for twenty minutes, fell into a swoon and then tried to run in four directions at once,' which is how it would be with you or me. Farmers simply don't feel pain – that little voice in your head that tells you not to do something because it's foolish and will hurt like hell and for the rest of your life somebody will have to cut up your food for you doesn't speak to them. My grandfather was just the same. He would often be repairing the car when the jack would slip and he would call out to you to come and crank it up again as he was having difficulty breathing, or he would run over his foot with the lawn-mower, or touch a live wire, shorting out the whole of Winfield but leaving himself unscathed apart from a ringing in the ears and a certain lingering smell of burnt flesh. Like most people from the rural Midwest, he was practically indestructible. There are only three things that can kill a farmer: lightning, rolling over in a tractor, and old age.

Mississippi

It is easy to misunderstand somebody if their accent is different from yours. And mistakes are more likely to happen if you are extremely nervous, as Bill Bryson was when he was waiting at traffic lights in Senatobia, Mississippi, and a dangerous-looking state trooper pulled up beside him.

He was sweaty and overweight and sat low in his seat. I assume he was descended from the apes like all the rest of us, but clearly in his case it had been a fairly gentle slope.

I stared straight ahead with a look that I hoped conveyed seriousness of purpose mingled with a warm heart and innocent demeanour. I could *feel* him looking at me. At the very least I expected him to gob a wad of tobacco juice down the side of my head. Instead, he said, 'How yew doin'?'

This so surprised me that I answered, in a cracking voice, 'Pardon?'

'I said how yew doin'?'

'I'm fine' I said. And then added, having lived some years in Britain, 'Thank you.'

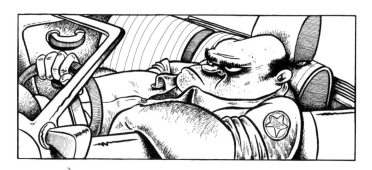

'Y'on vacation?'

'Yup.'

'Hah doo lack Miss Hippy?'

'Pardon?'

'I say, Hah doo lack Miss Hippy?'

I was quietly distressed. The man was armed and Southern and I couldn't understand a word he was saying to me. 'I'm sorry,' I said, 'I'm kind of slow, and I don't understand what you're saying.'

'I say' – and he repeated it more carefully – 'how doo yew *lack* Mississippi?'

It dawned on me. 'Oh! I like it fine! I like it heaps! I think it's wonderful. The people are so friendly and helpful.' I wanted to add that I had been there for an hour and hadn't been shot at once, but the light changed and he was gone, and I sighed and thought, 'Thank you, Jesus.'

Activities

A hanging

1 It is often the choice of details in George Orwell's descriptions that makes them especially powerful. For example, in 'A hanging', he allows you to imagine exactly what the prisoner looks like by focusing on his over-large moustache, 'rather like the moustache of a comic man on the films'.

    a In pairs, talk about the way he uses details in this account. For example:

- What comparison does he use to describe the way the guards hold the man after he has been brought out of his cell?
- What impression do we get of the jail superintendent?
- How does Orwell represent the way Francis, the head jailer, speaks; and how does his way of speaking help to give an impression of his character?

    b Which small detail starts Orwell thinking about 'what it means to destroy a healthy, conscious man'? Why do you think it has that effect on him?

2 Write the jail superintendent's official report of the hanging. Give it a date in 1930 and invent a name for the jail. Include incidents that were different from the usual routine, such as Francis's lateness and the incident with the dog. You could end: 'The execution was successfully carried out at 8.08.' Remember that it is an official report - use short sentences and formal language.

A sniper in the trenches

3 Throughout this account, George Orwell talks about other people in a highly impersonal way. He refers to them as: 'another man', 'Fascists', 'a man', 'an officer'. This only changes when he talks about a messenger holding up his trousers while running along the parapet of a trench. He refers to this man as 'a fellow human being'. Why do you think he does this?

4 In pairs, talk about the three reasons George Orwell gives for not shooting the enemy soldier. In particular, try to explain the third reason.

5 Write George Orwell's official report when he gets back to base. Give information about the terrain, the enemy positions and the air-raid. Your companion must have seen the enemy soldier running through the trenches holding his trousers up – how do you explain the fact that you did not shoot him?

The sporting spirit

6 Do you agree with Orwell's opinions about international sporting contests? Hold a class debate on whether or not international sport inevitably leads to conflict. You could refer to competitions that have happened recently.

7 Write an article in reply to Orwell's comments on 'the sporting spirit'. Put forward arguments in favour of international sporting contests such as the football World Cup and the Olympic Games, explaining their benefits.

At the barber's

8 In order to enjoy all the humour in Bill Bryson's account, there are things we have to understand. In pairs, explain the jokes behind:

   •   the way the barber occasionally mutters 'Oh, dang' or 'Whoopsie'

- the question 'How fast does your hair grow?'
- the question 'do you have a big hat?'
- the references to Barney Rubble and Hercules Poirot

- the barber's nickname, 'Thumbs'.

9 Write your own account of an experience in which you felt powerless, as Bill Bryson does at the barber's. For example, you could recount a parents' consultation evening at school (where you accompanied your parents), or a visit to the dentist.

Farmers

10 Bill Bryson's comments on farmers are funny because we know that many of his statements are either exaggerations or downright lies. For example, we know that he is not speaking the literal truth when he says at the beginning that most farmers 'have parts missing off them'. (It must be true that some farmers have lost limbs; but to say that most have is obviously untrue.) Make a list of the other exaggerations or untruths in the extract to do with:

- farmers in the Midwest over the age of twenty
- why they lose limbs
- pain
- the reactions of farmers who lose a limb
- Bryson's grandfather mending the car
- the things that can kill a farmer.

11 Write your own comments on a particular group of people, in the style of this article. For example, you could write about teachers, dentists or parents. Include deliberate exaggerations and lies for humorous effect.

Mississippi

12 Much of the humour in this extract comes from Bill Bryson's inability to understand the Mississippi state trooper's accent. He represents this accent phonetically, that is, by spelling the word as it is said, for example, 'How yew doin'?'.

a In pairs, read out the dialogue between Bryson and the state trooper, giving the full effect of the state trooper's accent.

b What is the local accent in your part of the country? Write a few lines of dialogue between two local people in which you represent the accent phonetically.

13 The scene between Bryson and the state trooper would work brilliantly on film. Create the screenplay for their exchange, using the dialogue and any other details that Bryson has given you. You could start off:

> **Shot 1:** Bryson's car stops at a red light. A state trooper's car pulls up alongside. Cut to –
>
> **Shot 2:** The interior of the state trooper's car: The state trooper looks across at Bryson. Cut to –
>
> **Shot 3:** The interior of Bryson's car: Bryson stares straight ahead, clearly nervous. Cut back to –
>
> **Shot 4:** (As for shot 2):

State trooper (chewing): How yew doin'?

Comparing the extracts

14 a Make notes on the features that Orwell's extracts have in common. For example, you could include the way he:

- writes about subjects which have a world-wide importance
- records facts
- focuses on details
- likes to use incidents in order to make a serious point
- writes about incidents from his past, or events in the news.

b Now do the same for Bryson's writing. You could include the way he:

- writes about ordinary, day-to-day subjects
- uses humour
- exaggerates
- writes about things that have happened to him
- likes to use dialogue.

Finally, note down (i) what the two writers have in common; and (ii) what the main differences are between them. When you have completed your notes, write an essay comparing the two writers. Use the notes you have made, and conclude by saying which of the two writers you prefer, and why.

Founding Editors: Anne and Ian Serraillier

Chinua Achebe Things Fall Apart
David Almond Skellig
Maya Angelou I Know Why the Caged Bird Sings
Margaret Atwood The Handmaid's Tale
Jane Austen Pride and Prejudice
Stan Barstow Joby: A Kind of Loving
Nina Bawden Carrie's War; The Finding; Humbug
Malorie Blackman Tell Me No Lies; Words Last Forever
Charlotte Brontë Jane Eyre
Emily Brontë Wuthering Heights
Melvin Burgess and Lee Hall Billy Elliot
Betsy Byars The Midnight Fox; The Pinballs; The Eighteenth Emergency
Victor Canning The Runaways
Sir Arthur Conan Doyle Sherlock Holmes Short Stories
Susan Cooper King of Shadows
Robert Cormier Heroes
Roald Dahl Danny; The Champion of the World; The Wonderful
Story of Henry Sugar; George's Marvellous Medicine; The Witches;
Boy; Going Solo; Matilda; My Year
Anita Desai The Village by the Sea
Charles Dickens A Christmas Carol; Great Expectations; A Charles
Dickens Selection
Berlie Doherty Granny was a Buffer Girl; Street Child
Roddy Doyle Paddy Clarke Ha Ha Ha
George Eliot Silas Marner
Anne Fine The Granny Project
Leon Garfield Six Shakespeare Stories
Ann Halam Dr Franklin's Island
Thomas Hardy The Withered Arm and Other Wessex Tales; The Mayor
of Casterbridge
Ernest Hemmingway The Old Man and the Sea; A Farewell to Arms
Barry Hines A Kestrel For A Knave
Nigel Hinton Buddy; Buddy's Song
Anne Holm I Am David

How many have you read?